Taekwondo Kyorugi
Olympic Style Sparring

Taekwondo Kyorugi
Olympic Style Sparring

2nd Edition

written by

Sang H. Kim, Ph.D.
Kuk Hyun Chung
Kyung Myung Lee

Turtle Press   Hartford

TAEKWONDO KYORUGI

Photographs courtesy of: WTF
                              Kuk Hyun Chung
                              Kyung Myung Lee
                              Sang H. Kim

To contact the authors or to order additional copies of this book:
      Turtle Press
      401 Silas Deane Hwy
      P.O. Box 290206
      Wethersfield, CT 06129-0206
      1-880-77-TURTL

Library of Congress Card Catalog Number 98-42159

ISBN 1-880336-24-3

Second English Language Edition

Library of Congress Cataloguing-in-Publication Data

Kim, Sang H.
        [T' aekwŏndo kyŏrugi. English]
        Taekwondo kyorugi : Olympic style sparring / written by Sang H.
    Kim, Kuk Hyun Chung, Kyung Myung Lee. -- 2nd ed. , 2nd English
    language ed.
        p.   cm.
        Rev. ed. of : Taekwondo kyorugi / written by Kuk Hyun Chung and
    Kyung Myung Lee. 1st English language ed. c1994
        Includes bibliographic references (p.) and index.
        ISBN 1-880336-24-3
        1. Tae kwon do. 2. Tae kwon do--Rules. 3. Tae kwon do--Competitions.
     I. Chung, Kuk Hyun. II. Lee, Kyung Myung. III. Chung, Kuk Hyun.
    T' aekwŏndo kyŏrugi. English. IV. Title.
    GV1114.9.K5413 1999
      796.815'3--dc21   98-42159

THE WORLD TAEKWONDO FEDERATION

635 YUKSAMDONG, KANGNAMKU
SEOUL, KOREA (135)
CABLE ADDRESS WORLD TAEKWONDO

A special message from President Un Yong Kim

June 1994

Taekwondo, which originated from Korea is now becoming a global sport. It is encouraging that this sport has become an official program of major multi-sport and continental games such as the Pan-Am Games, World Games, Goodwill Games, etc., making its value known to the whole world.

Athletes and coaches have to continuously train themselves for Taekwondo competition with both physical practice and study of the theories of taekwondo. Written materials for educating coaches and competitors are still not easy to access. I hope more documents of this nature will be published.

More research such as this should be made by Taekwondo practitioners and masters on the theorectical side of Taekwondo to increase its international popularity and make it an official Olympic sport. I commend Grandmaster Kyung Myung Lee, Master Sang Hwan Kim and Master Kuk Hyun Chung for their hard work toward the improvement of taekwondo and recommend this book be widely read by Taekwondo practitioners.

Dr. Un Yong Kim
President, WTF
Vice President, IOC

BEFORE YOU BEGIN

Exercises, advice and activities contained in this book are
intended for elite level (professional) athletes and competitors.
They are strenuous and may result in injury to the practitioner.
As with all exercise programs, consult a physician before
beginning.

Contents

Preface

Taekwondo originated over 2000 years ago in Korea. Now, in over 160 countries we hear the echoes of the dynamic kihap sound of taekwondo. Taekwondo is now a global sport and martial art. It has been contributing tremendously to the health and fitness of millions of practitioners for many years.

The World Taekwondo Federation, the official governing body of taekwondo, was formed in 1973. It was admitted into the General Association of the International Sports Federations (GAISF) and the International Olympic Committee (IOC) in 1980. Taekwondo debuted as an Olympic Demonstration Game in 1988 in Seoul, South Korea and was featured again in 1992 in Barcelona, Spain. In 2000, taekwondo is officially a full medal sport in the Summer Olympic Games.

With the rapid innovations brought about by the internationalization of competitive taekwondo, continuing research and publication is necessary to allow competitors in every country access to modern taekwondo skills and strategy. *Taekwondo Kyorugi* is a concise guide to competition for serious taekwondo competitors and instructors. The authors of this book have extensive experience in competing, coaching, and teaching at the highest levels of taekwondo. In writing this book, we have made great efforts to standardize the terminology and systematize the technical structure of competition training for the benefit of taekwondo competitors around the globe.

We hope *Taekwondo Kyorugi* will be a milestone for all taekwondo practitioners. Special thanks to Sung Hwan Chung and Sung Hee Lee and to Turtle Press which has greatly contributed to martial arts culture worldwide.

Kyung Myung Lee
Sang Hwan Kim
Kuk Hyun Chung

Chapter 1: Taekwondo Competition

Taekwondo is a traditional Korean martial art and modern combat sport practiced all over the world. It has been developed, as in the cases of boxing, wrestling, fencing and judo, as a one-on-one combat sport. Taekwondo was an Olympic demonstration game in Seoul, Korea in 1988 and Barcelona, Spain in 1992, with eight weight divisions. In 2000, taekwondo is a full medal sport (with four weight divisions) in the Olympic Games.

Taekwondo literally consists of three words:

Tae　(태) means a system of foot techniques
Kwon (권) means a system of hand techniques
Do　 (도) means the art of experiencing the
　　　　　　ultimate being through physical and
　　　　　　metaphysical enlightenment

Taekwondo practitioners can develop strong physical fitness and mental strength through basic techniques, poomse (form), Kyukpa (breaking), Machuo Kyorugi (arranged sparring), and Jayu Kyorugi (free sparring). Through practicing the spectrum of taekwondo skills the practitioner can prepare himself not only for competition but also for any life-threatening situations.

Taekwondo is a total fitness program. If *Taekwon* denotes the external form of the art, *Do* connotes the internal essence. The essence of Taekwondo begins from the spirit of martial arts. It is a way of improving the self through constant internal struggles between the negative self and the positive one.

To achieve the highest state of the mind, it is necessary for taekwondo practitioners to experience constant battles between the real self and the illusive self, the right way and the wrong way. To help further this process, meditation is frequently used. Meditation is an essential element in attaining the highest state of mind. The main goal of meditation is the attainment of enlightenment. The result of this combination of physical and mental training is the cultivation of character and the discovery of the ideal path in life. The ultimate answer to what Taekwondo is can be defined as a *philosophical activity through which the practitioner can attain the highest level of unity of the body, mind, and spirit.*

"The ultimate winner is the one who can conquer himself. Kyorugi is a fight within the self. The one who can win over himself can eventually win over the opponent."

Kyorugi and Competition

Kyorugi is an actual fight between two competitors using the offensive and defensive skills acquired through the practice of Taekwondo. There are two types of Kyorugi as defined by the degree of limitation of the skills allowed. They are machuo kyorugi (arranged sparring) and jayu kyorugi (free sparring). Jayu kyorugi is the form of sparring that is implemented in Taekwondo competition.

Valid techniques for scoring points in competition include a variety of punching and kicking skills. The punch can be used only to the trunk (areas covered by the chest guard) and kicking techniques can be executed to the face (head, in front of the ears) and trunk (areas covered by the chest guard). Any technique below the belt is prohibited. One point is awarded to a technique that is delivered accurately on a legal area with the proper amount of power. To score a valid point, an attack must be acknowledged by two or more judges or be recorded by the electronic chest protector depending on the scoring system in use and the target of the attack. The winner is decided by points or knock out. If case of a tie, the winner is decided by the rule of superiority.

Illegal techniques and behavior are penalized by a warning (kyung-go) or deduction of a point (gam-jeom). The accumulation of two warnings by a competitor results in the deduction of one point. The competitor who accumulates three deduction points, by kyung-go or gam-jeom penalties, throughout the match is automatically disqualified.

Most of the vital points of the legal target areas are shielded by protection gear worn by the competitors. It is mandatory for all competitors to wear head gear, a chest protector, shin guards, forearm guards, and a groin protector to prevent potential injuries.

Taekwondo competition takes place on the 26' x 26' mat between two competitors identified by the color of their chest protectors as blue (chung) and red (hong). Adult competitors are divided by weight and gender into sixteen divisions for international competition or eight divisions for Olympic competition. Junior competitors are divided by weight and gender into 20 divisions for international competition. (see *Chapter 14: WTF Competition Rules* at the back of this book for official adult and junior weight classes) A standard international match consists of three rounds of three minutes with a one minute break between rounds.

The match is officiated by a referee and three judges if electronic scoring equipment is not used or a referee and two judges if electronic scoring equipment is used.

The Spirit of Competition

As in the Olympic slogan of "Faster, Higher, and Stronger," taekwondo competition encourages competitors to improve the level of human capacity. Taekwondo competition is a form of education that takes place through the practice of skills and their application in competition, based on traditional values. The fundamental significance of taekwondo competition lies in the fact that the competition ring provides a venue where following the rules and doing one's best are rewarded. The site of competition is a place to learn the way to achieve harmony and perfection of the mind, body and spirit through the discovery of the true self. This is possible through the struggle within the self and against the opponent.

Competition is a method of developing the full potential of the human body, both physically and technically. Taekwondo competition pursues the development and integration of fitness, technique and strategy as well as a sense of humility and sportsmanship.

The ultimate ideal of taekwondo practice is to achieve a state of mind in which the performer is acutely aware of the endlessly changing competition environment and can effortlessly react to such changes. This state of mind becomes possible through the mastery of a broad range of offensive and defensive taekwondo skills.

Development of Competition

From ancient times, taekwondo has been practiced as a form of self-defense on both the individual and national levels. During the Japanese colonial period in Korea (1910-1945), the Japanese government prohibited traditional Korean martial arts training to prevent antigovernment uprising by the Korean people. After liberation from the Japanese on August 15, 1945, the elders of the Korean martial arts community met to revive the traditional, preoccupation arts. Because of these efforts, the Korea Taekwondo Association (KTA) was formed in 1961.

In 1963, taekwondo was accepted as an official event in the 43rd National Athletic Festival marking the official debut of taekwondo as a national sport. Since the early 1960's, many Korean taekwondo instructors have taken up residence throughout the world, promoting taekwondo in their new home countries. Because of this, taekwondo has enjoyed global popularity as an international sport. This trend has also been marked by the ascent of kyorugi as the main area of practice for taekwondo competitors.

In 1973, the first World Taekwondo Championship was held in Seoul, Korea with eighteen participating countries. At this time, the World Taekwondo Federation (WTF) was formed to support the worldwide taekwondo movement in a more structured way. Since 1973, the World Taekwondo Championship has been held every two years, with 1987 marking the first time women's competition divisions were included.

The headquarters of the WTF is located at Kukkiwon in Seoul, Korea. The WTF is the official international governing body for taekwondo and has a membership of over 160 countries. It is now recognized by both the International Olympic Committee (IOC) and the General Association of the International Sports Federations (GAISF). Under the auspices of these and other regional organizations, taekwondo is included in many international, regional and national sporting events.

Timeline of Modern Taekwondo

Sept. 16, 1961	Korea Taekwondo Association (KTA) formed
Feb. 23, 1963	Taekwondo accepted into Korea Athletic Assoc.
Nov. 30, 1972	Kukkiwon, headquarters of taekwondo, built
May 25, 1973	1st Men's World Taekwondo Championship
May 28, 1973	World Taekwondo Federation (WTF) formed
Oct. 18, 1974	1st Asian Taekwondo Championship held
Oct. 5, 1975	Recognized by GAISF
Apr. 9, 1976	Recognized by Conseil Internationale du Sports Militaire (CISM)
July 17, 1980	Recognized by International Olympic Committee (IOC)
July 3, 1986	1st World Cup Taekwondo Championship
Sept. 30, 1986	Accepted as an official sport in Asian Games
Nov. 29, 1986	1st World Collegiate Taekwondo Championship
Aug. 9, 1987	Accepted as an official sport in Pan-Am Games
Oct. 7, 1987	1st Women's World Taekwondo Championship
Sept. 17, 1988	Olympic demonstration games held, Korea
July. 30, 1992	Olympic demonstration games held, Spain
September, 2000	Full medal sport at Olympic Games, Australia

Taekwondo demonstration at the 1988 Olympic Games in Seoul

Official International Taekwondo Events

International Championships

♦ World Taekwondo Championships
♦ World Cup
♦ FISU (World Collegiate Championship)
♦ CISM (World Military Championship)

Regional Championships

♦ Asian Taekwondo Championship
♦ European Taekwondo Championship
♦ Pan-Am Taekwondo Championship
♦ African Taekwondo Championship
♦ Southeast Asian Taekwondo Championship
♦ Middle Eastern Taekwondo Championship
♦ Mediterranean Cup Taekwondo Championship

Multi-sport/Continental Championships

♦ Olympic Games (2000)
♦ Olympic Demonstration Games (1988, 1992)
♦ World Games
♦ Pan-Am Games
♦ Central American Sports Games
♦ Caribbean Games
♦ All-Africa Games
♦ Asian Games (1986, 1994)
♦ Southeast Asian Games
♦ South American Games
♦ Goodwill Games

Chapter 2:
Essence of Kyorugi

Kyorugi means competition among two or more contestants to prove who is the best through physical prowess and technical excellence. For Kyorugi it requires at least two people to stand against each other. Since Kyorugi requires every possible means to defeat the opponent within the permissible rules, you must have mastered the fundamentals skills before you enter the Kyungijang (competition site).

Within the designated place and time, the contestants attack and counterattack using the hands and feet. Quick reflexes and agility are the most fundamental attributes that Kyorugi competitors should have for his or her safety and success in the competition.

The most idealistic Kyorugi is a perfectly harmonized performance of attack and counterattack in perfect timing. Through Kyorugi practice, you can accomplish two important things: the ability to control your body the way you want in any moment and the ability to liberate yourself to be who you want to be. It helps you experience the status of self-actualization. It is a process that formulates the integration of the external and internal aspects of the self, leading to the complete unity of the mind and body.

Fundamental Kyorugi Principles

Kyorugi is an activity that requires total integration of human potential. The foremost element is your physical fitness. No matter how well you are prepared technically, it is impossible to make your dream come true unless you are physically fit. But, with excellent fitness alone, it is still impossible to compete successfully. You must have technical superiority and strategy of how to use your techniques. When things get rough, your final dependence would be on your fighting spirit that helps you go on against odds. Now let's take look at those element

1. Fitness

Kyorugi fitness includes strength, power, speed, endurance, and flexibility. Quality power is generated by the strength of quality muscles. For endurance, you need to develop slow twitch muscles through aerobic exercises. For speed, you need to develop fast twitch muscle fibers through anaerobic or interval training. (For a more detailed explanation, refer to the book *Ultimate Fitness Through Martial Arts,* Turtle Press, ISBN 1-880336-02-2)

2. Technique

There are 11 fundamental Taekwondo techniques in this book, that are commonly used in the competition. They are roundhouse kick, back kick, axe kick, side kick, whip kick, spin whip kick, pushing kick, crescent kick, punch, front kick, and double kick. Once the fundamentals are sufficiently mastered, you must comprehend the unique characteristic of each technique. The examples are linear or circular, short or long, forward or backward movement, etc. Then the timing, tempo, and rhythm of the techniques in continuous action must be understood for perfect execution.

3. Strategy

The foremost principle for developing strategy is to know your strengths and weaknesses. Then you must have as much information as possible about the opponent. Use your footwork or feinting motions and feel out the way your opponent reacts. Find out whether your opponent is an offensive or defensive style fighter. Then discover what his favorite techniques are. Once you find the characteristics of the opponent, lead the game in the way you can play best. In order not to expose your weakness or tactics, it is necessary for you to prepare a variety of techniques and tactical combinations.

4. Fighting Spirit

A weak mind turns a strong body into a coward. A strong mind makes even a physically weak body function better than it could perform otherwise. When you have a strong mind and strong body, no one can stop you. Fighting spirit is the trigger that makes the ordinary mind extraordinary. The fighting spirit can only be developed through the experience of going through numerous hardships in the training process. The tougher the training is the stronger the spirit can become. To capture the chance that passes in a split second, your spirit should be as clear as crystal and as strong as a hurricane. Your fighting spirit is what makes your technique work even in the toughest situation.

Kyorugi Attributes

Kyorugi attributes are the qualities that cause you to perform successfully. They are more internal than techniques. They can be compared to flavors in cooking, which enable many different ingredients to contribute their unique taste toward one goal.

1. Ability to Assess the Opponent

Before you launch your own fighting plan, you must know the style and habits of your opponent as much as possible. If you keep making the same mistakes in your fight, it means you are not sure of who your opponent is. When the fight begins, make sure you analyze the following things:
   1) Is the opponent aggressive style or countering style?
   2) Is the opponent front leg or rear leg kicking style?
   3) What are the favorite techniques of the opponent?

2. Total Coordination

In Taekwondo competition, kicking is the main weapon. However, the importance of the upper body should not be ignored for two reasons. The frequent usage of the upper body, particularly the arms, is a necessity to achieve total equilibrium of the body in motion. Without proper maneuvering of the upper body, there is no perfect balance of the lower body.

The second reason is that arms are the best weapon to use for defense in close fighting. Adequate defensive action using the arms often creates opportunities for you to attack or stop the opponent's continuous attacking. Therefore, the balance between upper and lower body should be part of your daily practice.

3. Distance Control

Read the distance. Every fighter has different distance concepts according to his habit, the length of the legs, training methods, strategies, or speed. The fundamental method of controlling the distance is to fully utilize your quick footwork. Practice how to always position your center at the spot from which you can punch or kick at any time. Since the distance constantly changes, your perception should be developed enough to take action or react to adjust to those changes. Both your hands and feet should be synchronized to act as one unit. In close fight, your speed must be superior in order to survive the exchange of blows. The bottom line in controlling the distance is to identify your attacking distance while your opponent constantly moves and to conceal it from your opponent.

1) Attack when you have the right distance. The best defensive tactic is to attack. In taekwondo kyorugi, attacking is defending and defending is attacking. In another words, you should not think of the two concepts as two. They must be integrated into one. Your attacking is a direct defensive activity and your countering is also a part of the attack against your opponent's aggression. In order to achieve this Oneness, you must develop your timing.

2) Change the distance to disrupt the opponent's attacking rhythm. Your footwork moves like a wave in the ocean: moving in and out. The wave creates a natural rhythm. It is a spatial wave of energy. Whoever controls it can determine who is going to win in that fight. In practice, develop fast attacking footwork and fast retreating footwork. Attack swiftly and retreat quickly. When you spot the chance to attack, follow your rhythm and drive the opponent into the corner. When your opponent figures out what you are doing and tries to begin his attack, move out swiftly and do not give the right distance for an attack. Let him miss the target. Then you can succeed in attacking and counterattacking.

3) Develop your own footwork: According to your size and fighting style, you should develop your own best way of doing the footwork. By proficient footwork, you can feint out the opponent or create an opening in the opponent's attacking movement. Good footwork is a must for short fighters. Good footwork brings out not only the natural flow of combination skills for attacking but also excellent timing for counterattacking.

4. Emotional Control

Everyone worries before a fight. No one is free from the fear of engaging in combat. You will surely begin to doubt your own skills when things go against your plan. To cure this disease, there is only one method: daily engagement in intensive training that strengthens your mind and body until every action comes automatically without conscious thought. When you begin to lose, it is easy for you to become emotional. You are apt to be anxious to score points to catch up. If you are in a hurry, you lose the balance of your mind and your anxiousness blinds you. The outcome is sure to be failure. Therefore, it is important to practice how to be cool in the middle of chaos in your daily practice.

5. Timing

Timing is synchronization of your execution of the technique with the opportunity that is given in front of you. It is a matter of an effective choice of time. Bad timing means a bad performance. No matter how perfect your personal techniques are, if they don't synchronize with the situation, they won't work. Since every technique has a different timing, you should carefully study the nature of individual skills so that your body can naturally sense the flow of each technique. At the same time, you should study different timing of different fighters. The first thing you should develop is a sharp visual sense to spot the opportunity. The second is an accurate and almost instinctive judgement to choose the right reaction. The third element is to develop the right kind and proportion of the muscles that are required for specific techniques.

6. Rhythm

In fighting, there are changes and flows that carry the changes. This flow is a rhythm. The changes are mostly visible, but the flow is not a visible thing. To win you must create the winning rhythm. You must keep a close eye on the opportunities and not miss them. When you miss them, you lose the rhythm. The other side of it is that you should let your opponent miss it and destroy his rhythm. When you attack, do it like a prey-attacking-eagle; when you retreat do like a running mouse fleeing the chasing cat. To control the rhythm of the game, identify the rhythm of the opponent and let him be comfortable with that. Then, you can break his rhythm with a faster technique or irregular rhythm approach.

7. Agility

Agility is the ability to change direction or body position quickly and proceed smoothly with another movement. Agility is physical intelligence. Essentially, agility is a smoothly integrated combination of perception, coordination, speed, strength, and balance (p.131, *Ultimate Fitness through Martial Arts*). When you perform a group of combination skills, they should be linked together quickly and coherently. Agility provides that link. Agility is also important in responding quickly and correctly to an opponent. Skillful evasion and footwork are based on moving swiftly and changing direction frequently in response to the opponent's actions.

8. Perception

Perception is the ongoing cerebral process of organizing and giving meaning to sensory input. Your perception of situations determines the responses that you make to the events. It is a basic requirement for the acquisition of physical skills. By accurately organizing and defining incoming information, you can translate the situation into a physical action. Therefore, learning the right technique in the right way is critical to be effective fighter. When you have a low level of perception skills, you may observe and respond to only the most obvious sensory cues. So in your daily training, include complex skill practice so your brain can organize and respond to hundreds of minute details with accuracy, particularly in the heat of the competition.

9. Power

Power is a combination of strength and explosiveness. Maximum power is created by releasing maximum muscular force at maximum speed. To increase power, you must increase both speed and strength. In taekwondo kyorugi, the ability to strike with power is critical in creating a trembling impact on the opponent to score a point. Then where does power come from? Power is derived from muscular ability. The human body contains nearly 400 muscles that can be broken in two classes: smooth and striated. Smooth muscles are those that perform the involuntary functions of the body including circulation and digestion. Striated muscles are those that can be voluntarily contracted, such as the muscle groups in the arms and legs.

You can strengthen by either isometric or isotonic exercises. Normal muscle movement is isotonic. One muscle lengthens while the other contracts in complementary pairs. A good example is weight training. As you lift the weight and then return it to its original position, your muscles lengthen and contract alternately through the full range of motion. Isometric exercise is to lift the same weight but it should not move. No matter how hard you work it remains in the same place. The muscular response you experience when applying force against an immovable object such as this is an isometric contraction. The key to effective and consistent strength gains is to apply the proper amount of stress in the correct way at the proper frequency.

10. Strategic Thinking

The foremost strategy in kyorugi is that attacking brings a better chance to win than merely being defensive. Good attacking skills with perfect timing bring you the advantages of scoring a point and leading the game. However, any attacking attempt that misses the target exposes a vulnerability of you, which causes your opponent to counterattack against your movement. So before engaging in an attacking strategy, fully understand the various defensive techniques against general and surprise attacks from your opponent.

The second strategic thinking is that attacking is the best defense. In a fast paced kyorugi match, often it is impossible to separate the time of attack from the one of defense. There are many simultaneous techniques that are used for offensive and defensive purposes in kyorugi techniques. Successful attacks make the opponent powerless. Successful attacks discourage your opponent to attempt initiative attacks.

11. Sense of Perspective

Your action in kyorugi should be reasonable and strategic and yet instinctive. If you are too occupied in what your opponent tries to do to you, you might miss out what he really plans to do against you such as set-up. You must be able to keep your outlook on the game without loosing the emotional balance particularly when you lose points. Do not be over-attached to the thought of winning. It will make your muscles tight. Do not worry about the consequences or fear of injury or losing. It will disturb your respiratory cycle. Focus your mind on each moment without being distracted by your own inner thoughts. Don't worry about your weakness once you are in the ring. Utilize your weakness as a hook to lure in your opponent. During training sessions, analyze every technique that you are going to use in the competition. Develop your way of performing so that you can maximize your strength and use the weakness to achieve your ultimate goal. This process will bring you confidence that keeps you balanced.

Chapter 3: Competition Skills

Technical proficiency in taekwondo competition cannot be attained by chance. It can only be achieved through the consistent effort of the competitor and his or her coach, trainer or instructor. Taekwondo competition is designed to be a direct contest of skills between two opponents in which the outcome appears to be determined by the power and accuracy of each competitor's skills.

However, at the highest levels of competition, an acute sense of strategy and discerning technique selection are required to outmaneuver and defeat the opponent. Based on the basic skills of taekwondo, each competitor, along with his or her coach, must develop a unique method of attack and counterattack that is best suited to his or her style.

Since the ultimate goal of competition is to defeat the opponent, each competitor must cultivate certain characteristics that are essential for achieving victory. The most fundamental attributes of every competitor include skillful technique, physical and mental fitness, strategy, agility and innate aestheticism. Beyond these fundamentals, perennial champions demonstrate the consistent ability to improve and adapt their skills and strategy and to perform well under pressure.

Components of a Competitor

Limited ability factors

1. General factors
   a. speed
   b. flexibility
   c. coordination

2. Athletic skill factors
   a. offense skills
   b. countering skills
   c. footwork

3. Mental factors
   a. motivation
   b. self-awareness
   c. self-control
   d. concentration
   e. strategy

Decisive ability factors

1. Mental factors
   a. general intellect
   b. mental training and others

2. General physical factors
   a. endurance
   b. agility
   c. power

3. Physical structural factors
   a. symmetry
   b. height

Techniques

Taekwondo techniques can be viewed as a means of resolving the situations presented in competition. Through proper analysis of each situation, the competitor can select and apply the correct attack or counterattack, resulting in the neutralization of the opponent and thereby achieving the necessary objective. The ability to size up and quickly react to the given situation is very important in advancing in competition.

To be able to apply the necessary skills, each skill must be thoroughly understood through a process of learning, practicing and eventually mastering it. At the advanced level, taekwondo skills become increasingly complex and require a highly specialized level of fitness especially flexibility, power, coordination, agility and reflexes.

There are many competition skills available to the taekwondo competitor. The most commonly used skills include:

1. Punching (jirugi) using the two foreknuckles
    a. straight middle punch
    b. angular middle punch

2. Kicking (chagi) using the foot below the ankle
    a. roundhouse kick
    b. back kick
    c. axe kick
    d. spin whip kick
    e. whip kick
    f. side kick
    g. front kick
    h. turning kick

3. Footwork (baljitgi) through strategic stepping
    a. forward footwork
    b. backward footwork
    c. lateral footwork
    d. turning footwork
    e. drawing footwork

4. Blocking (maki) using the hand and arm
   a. direct block
   b. indirect block

5. Feinting (sogimsu) using deceptive gestures
   a. footwork feinting
   b. body feinting
   c. motion feinting

The difference between competition taekwondo and martial taekwondo lies in the limitations placed on the range of applicable skills. In competition, the legal targets, for which the competitor may be awarded a point, include the head and trunk (see *Chapter 14: Competition Rules* for specific target areas). Therefore, the competitor must always be conscious of these targets and select techniques which result in the scoring of a point against such targets.

1. Fighting Stance (Kyorumsae)

Kyorumsae is an abbreviation of kyorugi and jasae. Kyorugi means fighting or sparring and jasae means stance. Kyorumsae, therefore, indicates the position the fighter assumes in preparation to fight.

The competitor must practice a correct fighting stance from the early stages of training. The appearance of the fighting stance differs according to the individual fighter's body structure and personal preference. Most fighting stances change according to the situation, including whether the fighter is in an offensive or defensive posture and whether he is preparing to move or has just finished a movement.

A good fighting stance is composed of:

1) Flexibility
A good stance allows for smooth, continuous movement by maintaining flexibility of posture.

2) Natural body posture
A good stance allows the body to act and react spontaneously, without undue hindrance.

3) Agility
A good stance allows for movement in any direction at split second intervals.

4) Base
A good stance requires a wide enough base (the distance between the feet) to maintain balance in movement and at rest.

5) Center of gravity
A good stance maintains the proper placement of the center of gravity, higher for rapid movements and lower for powerful movements.

6) Concealment
A good stance allows the fighter to hide the intention and initiation of offensive movements.

1) Standard fighting stance (kyorumsae)

The standard fighting stance, also called the front fighting stance, is the most fundamental stance in sparring. Based on the position of the rear foot, the standard stance is classified as either right handed or left handed. When the right foot is in the rear, it is a right handed stance and when the left foot is in the rear, it is a left handed stance. To make the standard fighting stance, position your feet at 1½ or 2 times your regular stride and turn your body approximately 45° to the side. From this stance, the execution of every taekwondo technique is possible.

2) Side fighting stance (yup-kyorumsae)

The side fighting stance is a variation of the standard fighting stance. The distance between the feet is slightly wider and the body is turned completely to the side. Side fighting stance is good for executing side kick and back kick.

3) Low fighting stance (natchoomsae)

The low fighting stance is second variation of the standard fighting stance. The distance between the feet is the same as in the side fighting stance and the body position is between that of the standard and side stances. The knees are bent lower than in the other stances and the upper body can lean slightly forward. Low fighting stance is good for counterattacking, especially with roundhouse kick and spin whip kick.

When considering the relationship of the fighters' stances, there are two possible configurations, open stance and closed stance.

1) Open stance (yullimsae)

Open stance suggests that the targets of the head and trunk are "open" to the opponent. Open stance is created when one fighter is in a left handed stance and the other is in a right handed stance.

2) Closed stance (datchimsae)

Closed stance suggests that the targets of the opponent are   hidden or "closed" to attack. Closed stance is created when both fighters concurrently assume a right handed or left handed stance.

2. Fundamental Offense Techniques

The offensive arsenal of taekwondo skills is made up of kicks and punches. Because of their longer attacking range and greater potential for power, kicks are the preferred attacks of taekwondo fighters. In traditional taekwondo, impacting with the ball, edge or heel of the foot is the prescribed method of kicking. However, in sport taekwondo the instep and bottom of the foot are the primary weapons for kicking.

1) Roundhouse kick (dollyo-chagi)

The roundhouse kick is the most frequently used kick in taekwondo because of its high rate of accuracy and simplicity. To execute the roundhouse kick, first chamber the knee and simultaneously pivot 180° on the supporting leg. Using the instep, strike to the face, stomach or rib/kidney area.

2) Back kick (dui-chagi)

Back kick is preferred for counterattacking, when there is less risk in turning the back to the opponent. In initiative attacking, the back kick should be long and penetrating, while for counterattacking it must be short and quick. To execute the back kick, pivot on the front foot while chambering the back leg. Quickly look over the turning shoulder at the opponent's movement. Turn the body slightly toward the target while the kicking foot passes by the supporting knee in a direct line to the target. Keep the upper body erect during the execution for maximum efficiency. The target for back kick is the trunk.

3) Axe kick (naeryo-chagi)

Axe kick has two main variations, bent knee kicking and straight knee kicking. To execute the bent knee axe kick, chamber the knee and unfold it in a downward direction, beginning at the highest point of the kicking trajectory. To execute the straight knee axe kick, lift the leg straight up at a slightly off center angle and drop it on the target. Both kicks can be used as inside kicking or outside kicking, defined by the relative position of your leg to the opponent's body. The striking surface of the foot is the sole or heel and the target is the face.

4) Whip kick (hooryo-chagi)

The whip kick can be executed with the lead or rear leg. For the lead leg whip kick, chamber the leg in front of the body and release it in a circular motion. For the rear leg whip kick, the body must first turn 180 degrees to chamber the leg in front. The sole of the foot is used to strike the face.

5) Spin whip kick (dui-hooryo-chagi)

The spin whip kick must be executed quickly and accurately to be efficient and powerful. To execute the spin whip kick, pivot on the front leg and chamber the rear leg. As the body spins around, release the kicking leg in a circular motion. During the spinning movement, quickly look at opponent over the turning shoulder. The sole of the foot is used to strike the face.

6) Side kick (yup-chagi)

The side kick is most effective when used as a front leg attack from the side stance. Chamber the leg and thrust it toward the target in a direct linear movement. The sole or edge of the foot is used to strike the trunk.

7) Pushing kick (mirro-chagi)

The pushing kick is used as a feint or a setup before the main attack. Pushing kick can be executed with the rear leg or the lead leg. Chamber the kicking knee slightly and quickly push toward the waist of the opponent with the sole of the foot.

8) Punch (jirugi)

Punching is used as a counterattack or as a tool to create space for follow-up kicks. When the push is accurately and powerfully delivered by the foreknuckles of the fist to the opponent's trunk it can score a point.

9) Front kick (ahp-chagi)

The front kick is rarely used in competition because the potential for injury to the ball of the foot and toes is great. To execute the front kick, chamber the knee and simultaneously thrust the foot to the target in a linear motion. The ball of the foot is used to strike the trunk and face.

10) Jump kick (tuiuh-chagi)

All of the basic kicking skills of taekwondo can be executed as jumping kicks as well. However, the longer you stay in the air while jumping, the more opportunity you provide the opponent for a counterattack. In competition, jumping kicks are generally used as short counterattacking techniques. When employed as an initiative attack, the jump is used to close the distance and penetrate the opponent's defenses rather than to achieve height.

11) Single leg combination kick (eeuh-chagi)

A single leg combination kick, two kicks with the same leg, requires great speed and technical proficiency. The striking surface and targets vary according to the type of kick. Examples of single leg combination kicks include middle section roundhouse kick followed by high section roundhouse kick and axe kick followed by side kick.

12) Double kick (doobal-dangsung-chagi)

A combination kick is executed by jumping and performing two kicks, one with each leg, before landing. It requires speed and advanced technical proficiency. The striking surface and target can vary with the type of kicks used. The two kicks may be the same type (e.g., two roundhouse kicks) or different (e.g. twisting kick and side kick).

3. Footwork (jitgi)

Footwork is an indirect skill used to set up a scoring technique. Footwork changes according to the opponent's stance, position, distance and the situation. The goals of footwork are:

1. to disrupt the opponent's offensive strategy
2. to avoid being attacked
3. to create a weakness in the opponent's movements
4. to create an opening in the opponent's defense
5. to launch an accurate and timely attack.

Tips for successful footwork:

1. Shift the body smoothly and lightly.
2. Synchronize the entire body as one unit.
3. Maintain equilibrium throughout every movement.
4. Adapt the stance according to the technique.

An example of footwork combined with kicking: slide forward and follow with roundhouse kick to the midsection.

Types of Footwork

Using a variety of footwork is an essential skill in taekwondo. Footwork is classified into five types according to the direction and structure of movement of the feet.

1) Forward footwork (naga-jitgi)

There are two types of forward footwork: *forward step*, in which the rear foot steps forward and the front foot acts as pivot and *forward slide*, in which both feet slide forward maintaining the same stance. The function of forward footwork is to shorten the distance to the opponent and secure the position that is best for attacking. Forward footwork is best followed by roundhouse kick or back kick.

Forward slide followed by a back kick.

2) Backward footwork (moollo-jitgi)

There are two types of backward footwork: *backward step*, in which the front foot steps back and the rear foot acts as pivot and *backward slide*, in which both feet slide backward maintaining the same stance. Backward footwork is best followed by roundhouse kick, back kick, and spin whip kick.

Using a backward slide to avoid an axe kick.

3) Lateral footwork (beekyo-jitgi)

There are two types of lateral footwork: *lateral pivot*, in which the rear foot moves at a forty-five degree angle to right or left while the front foot acts as pivot and *lateral slide*, in which both feet simultaneously slide to the right or left maintaining the same stance. Lateral footwork is best followed by an immediate counterattack, such as a roundhouse kick, axe kick or turn kick.

Lateral pivot.

4) Turning footwork (dwidora-jitgi)

Turning footwork indicates turning the body 180° forward to the posterior side by moving the rear foot and using the front foot as a pivot. The best techniques for turning are roundhouse, axe kick and whip kick.

An example of turning footwork.

5) Drawing footwork (kulro-jitgi)

There are two types of drawing footwork: the *front foot draw* in which the front foot is drawn along the ground toward the rear foot and *rear foot draw* in which the rear foot is drawn along the ground toward the front foot. Front drawing is especially effective when combined with a simultaneous rear leg roundhouse kick. Other kicks combined with drawing footwork are roundhouse kick, axe kick and whip kick.

An example of drawing footwork.

Sample combinations of footwork and kicking

Footwork	Kick	Target	Foot
Forward footwork	back kick roundhouse spin whip axe kick	trunk trunk/face face face	front/back " " "
Backward footwork	back kick roundhouse spin whip	trunk trunk/face face	front/back " "
Lateral footwork	roundhouse axe kick	trunk/face face	back "
Turning footwork	roundhouse whip kick spin whip	trunk/face face face	front " "
Drawing footwork	axe kick whip kick roundhouse	face face trunk/face	front " "

4. Combination Skills

A combination is a continuous attack that is comprised of at least two techniques. Combinations, like other skills, are largely developed based on personal style and preference. Beyond personal preference, there are several basic principles behind the development of combination techniques. First, the competitor must master single techniques such as roundhouse kick or back kick. Next, he must be able to combine these skills smoothly and apply them with the required footwork and feinting skills.

Examples of common combinations:
> a. right foot roundhouse kick to the trunk,
>   left foot roundhouse kick to the face
> b. right foot roundhouse kick to the trunk,
>   left foot back kick to the trunk
> c. right foot roundhouse kick to the trunk,
>   left foot roundhouse kick to the trunk
> d. left foot turn kick to the trunk,
>   right foot back kick to the trunk
> e. left foot axe kick to the face,
>   right foot roundhouse kick to the trunk

Combination A: Right foot roundhouse kick followed by left foot roundhouse kick

5. Defense Techniques

There are two types of defensive skills in taekwondo: direct defense and indirect defense. **Direct defense** means blocking a kick to the head or body by covering potential targets with the arm. An effective block prevents the opponent from scoring a point. There are two basic types of blocks: single block in which the forearm is used to cover the trunk or head area and double block in which one arm comes up to cover the head and the other drops to cover the trunk.

Indirect defense means avoiding an attack by moving out of its path using footwork or a change of stance. Indirect defense skills are usually followed by a counterattack. Counterattacking right after avoiding an attack is one of the most effective means of scoring in taekwondo competition.

A double block used against a high section roundhouse kick

6. Feinting Skills

A feint is an intentionally deceptive movement, intended to draw the opponent's attack and leave him open to a predetermined counterattack. The key to feinting is to deceive the opponent psychologically and cause him to misjudge the situation. A common feint is to make a front leg kicking motion and attack with a rear leg roundhouse kick or back kick.

Other types of feints are created through:
   a. body gestures that cause the opponent to lose his balance
   b. footwork that makes the opponent lose his sense of distance
   c. drawing that falsely causes the opponent to think there is a target open for him to attack easily.

The attacker uses a pushing kick to disrupt his opponent's distance and balance and then follows up with a jumping back kick to score.

Chapter 4:
Strategies

Strategy is a method to defeat the opponent through analysis of the situation, judgment of the available options and immediate execution of the most appropriate action. The purpose of using strategy is to manage the course of the match while conserving energy and moving wisely.

To execute an effective strategy in the match the fighter must be thoroughly familiar with the rules and regulations of the game, as well as the strategies in use by the current top international fighters, and have mastered fundamental skills that work in every situation. An excellent means of developing strategy is to watch and analyze international games on video tape. In the ring, the fighter also must be able to rely on his coach to evaluate the opponent and formulate strategy based on this evaluation.

Competition taekwondo is a game of strategy. The result of the match often hinges on the strategic proficiency of the competitors.

❖ 3 Considerations for Competition Strategy

1) *Technical structure and variations according to the competition rules.* Every competitor must be able to win within the established framework of the competition rules. He must create unique offensive combinations designed to score points while avoiding penalties.

2) *Economical use of energy over the duration of the match.* A fighter must plan his strategy over the course of the full nine minutes of the match. He must clearly decide when it is appropriate to conserve energy and when it is necessary to press the opponent.

3) *Judicial application of feinting skills.* Feinting should be used wisely and sparingly, so as not to be detected by the opponent.

The following process is necessary for the accurate formulation (psychological) and execution (physical) of strategy:

1. **Psychological formulation of strategy**
   a. concentration (attention to the opponent's every action)
   b. information collection (accumulation of information)
   c. data selection (sorting of the important information)
   d. analysis of the situation (projection of future events)
   e. decision making (selection of appropriate action)
   f. immediate execution (implementation of chosen action)

2. **Physical execution of strategy**
   g. adaptation (change of techniques according to situation)
   h. economic distribution of energy (conservation and assertion of energy at the proper time)
   i. timing (attack/defend appropriately)
   j. execution of plan (carry out planned strategy)
   k. score management (score enough points to win)

Offensive Strategy

Offense, in taekwondo competition, is the strategic application of skills to the target area of the opponent. It is most commonly applied with forward footwork and explosive movements. To be successful, offensive skills must be executed with good timing and an accurate sense of distance.

There are three methods of offense: direct attack, indirect attack and counterattack. A direct attack is an initiative attack, an indirect attack is a deceptive attack and a counterattack is a reflexive attack.

Direct attack

There are three types of direct attacks according to the *distance* and *stance* of the opponent.

1. The first is an **in-place attack** where the distance to the opponent is perfect for a single kicking attack and no footwork or deception is required.

2. The second is an **incline attack** where the distance is slightly beyond the reach of an in-place attack. Therefore the competitor must shift his body forward without moving his feet, and launch the attack from the inclined position. Timing, distance and speed are essential.

3. The third is a **sliding attack** where the distance is even greater than that of the incline attack. The competitor must slide his front foot in as he shifts his body weight forward to attack. Speed is essential for covering the distance in a sliding attack. For maximum efficiency, the competitor must execute the technique before the opponent recognizes his intention.

Indirect attack

There are three types of indirect attack: feinting, cutting and footwork.

1. **Feinting**: To create an opening, feint first and then attack according to the opponent's reaction.

2. **Cutting**: Cut the opponent's attacking movement and follow with a counterattack.

3. **Footwork**: According to the distance and stance of the opponent, initiate with footwork and attack.

Counterattack

There are two types of counter attacks: direct and indirect.

1. A **direct counterattack** means countering the opponent's attack without changing position. Speed, agility and fortitude are important for direct counterattacking.

2. An **indirect counterattack** means avoiding the opponent's attack with footwork and then following with a counterattack

---

Summary of Offensive Options:

1. Direct Attack
    a. in-place attack
    b. incline attack
    c. sliding attack
2. Indirect Attack
    a. feinting
    b. cutting
    c. drawing
3. Counterattack
    a. direct
    b. indirect

Strategic Tips for Winning

1. Counterattacking has a better chance of scoring than attacking for advanced competitors.

2. Beginning and intermediate competitors are most likely to score with single direct attacks.

3. In a close match, an attacking fighter is more likely to win that a counterattacking fighter unless the counterattacker can score a knockout.

4. The most frequently used attacks are roundhouse kick, back kick and axe kick. Successful competitors can effectively counter these kicks.

5. The side kick and front kick are rarely used in competition any more and are highly unlikely to score points.

6. The roundhouse kick is the preferred kick for scoring, followed by the back kick and axe kick.

7. Kicks to the trunk score points more frequently than kicks to the head.

8. Spin whip kick is the least likely kick (out of the frequently used kicks) to score.

9. The most productive round for scoring is the third round.

10. Although used frequently, punches are only likely to score a point if the opponent is felled by the punch.

11. Feinting should be used sparsely and only when there is an intention to attack.

12. Counter attacking fighters should capitalize on the use of their front leg to increase chances of scoring.

13. Occupying the center of the ring is most advantageous.

14. Whenever the opponent approaches the boundary line, push him out.

15. When the opponent positions himself in the corner, prepare to counter an aggressive attack.

16. When the referee says "Kaesok" attack immediately.

Assessing the Opponent

The goal of opponent assessment is to determine the opponent's:
    a. strategy
    b. technical skill
    c. mentality
    d. physical condition

This can be achieved by noting the following components:
    a. height
    b. stance
    c. fighting style
            ◆ infighter or outfighter
            ◆ attacker or counterattacker
    d. favorite skill
    e. psychological condition
    f. strength and weakness

Closing the distance with a direct attack.

Statistics for Formulating a Successful Strategy

Conclusions from Master Sang Jin Han, "Research of Frequency and Scoring Rate of Individual Skills of Taekwondo Competition," 1993 and Master Jae Bong Lee, "Analytical Research into Scoring Rate of Initiative Attack and Counter Attack of Taekwondo Competition," 1993

1. The **single attack** is used most frequently in competition because it can be executed from a stable stance.

2. A **counterattack** is good for scoring points because the competitor can wait for the perfect opportunity and attack while the opponent is off guard.

3. **Attacking** is more advantageous in competition because the rule of superiority states that in a tie, the more aggressive fighter wins.

4. **Counterattacking** has the highest success rate of any type of attack in terms of scoring points.

5. The **most frequently used kicks**, in descending order, are: roundhouse kick to the trunk, back kick to the trunk, axe kick to the face, roundhouse kick to the face, pushing kick to the trunk, punching to the trunk, spin whip kick to the face, front kick to the trunk, and side kick to the trunk.

6. The **kicks that score** most frequently, in descending order, are: roundhouse kick to the trunk, back kick to the trunk, roundhouse kick to the face, axe kick to the face, axe kick to the trunk, and spin whip kick to the face.

7. The kicks with the **highest of percentage of points** scored, (ratio of points scored to frequency of use) in descending order, are: back kick to trunk, roundhouse kick to face, roundhouse kick to the body, axe kick to the face, spin whip kick to the face, and pushing kick to the trunk.

Chapter 5: Professional Kyorugi Training

The goal of professional kyorugi training is to practice and perfect selected strategic techniques for use in actual competition. Professional training takes the competitor beyond the practice of basic movements and into the direct, successful application of skills as a whole unit. The goal of training is technical improvement and overall skill integration. This training must be done consistently throughout the competition preparation and competition season and should be geared toward maximum gains in the minimum amount of time.

Professional skill drills are a means of mastering the direct application of previously acquired techniques and strategy. The main focus of the training is the repeated drilling of the most frequently used advanced skills and their applications. There are five fundamental guidelines for implementing professional skill drills:

a. always use them at the beginning of the workout
b. schedule intensive repetition of skills
c. execute accurately with maximum power and speed
d. give full focus and conscious attention to performance
e. maintain supplementary physical training

Examples of Professional Skill Drills

1. Roundhouse kick (target: trunk)

- in-place rear leg roundhouse kick
- in-place multiple roundhouse kicks
- lead foot step in, roundhouse kick
- quick step, lead leg roundhouse kick
- in-place double roundhouse kick
- rear foot step back, double roundhouse kick
- in-place switch stance, roundhouse kick
- lead leg pushing kick, rear roundhouse kick
- rear leg roundhouse kick, return to same stance, same leg roundhouse kick
- lead leg feint, double roundhouse kick
- 360° spin (lead foot pivot), in-place roundhouse kick
- lead leg feint, front step in, roundhouse kick
- turn and side step, roundhouse kick
- switch stance, lead foot draw and roundhouse kick
- rear foot draw, roundhouse kick
- switch stance, lead leg roundhouse kick (trunk is fixed)

In-place, rear leg roundhouse kick

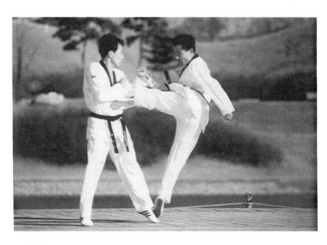

In-place, double roundhouse kick

2. Roundhouse kick (target: face)

- in-place roundhouse kick
- lead foot step in, roundhouse kick
- front foot draw, roundhouse kick
- rear hand punch, roundhouse kick

Lead foot step in, roundhouse kick

3. Back kick (target: trunk)

- in-place back kick
- lead foot step in, back kick
- switch stance, back kick
- rear foot step in, jumping back kick

In-place back kick

Rear foot step in, jumping back kick

4. Axe kick (target: face)

- rear leg axe kick
- lead leg axe kick, slide forward, lead leg axe kick
- lead leg jumping axe kick
- lead leg feint, simultaneous rear leg jump axe kick
- rear foot step back, lead leg axe kick

Lead leg jumping axe kick

5. Spin whip kick (target: face)

- ◆ in-place spin whip kick
- ◆ lead foot step in, spin whip kick
- ◆ slide back, spin whip kick
- ◆ in-place jumping spin whip kick
- ◆ step on the opponent's body, jumping spin whip kick

Step on the opponent's body, jumping spin whip kick

6. Counterattack

- slide back, roundhouse kick
- rear foot step back, lead leg roundhouse kick to face
- in-place lead leg roundhouse kick
- in-place lead leg axe kick
- slide back, double roundhouse kick
- in-place back kick
- in-place jumping back kick
- in-place spin whip kick
- in-place jumping spin whip kick
- slide back, jumping turn kick

In-place lead leg axe kick

Independent Training

When practicing alone, every technique can be practiced singly or in combination, at the individual's pace. The diverse stances and footwork of taekwondo can be combined with kicking skills, independently or in combinations, without the influence of a partner. By practicing independently, the fighter can practice a specific drill of his own rhythm, speed, skill level and physical condition. This type of practice is effective for perfecting advanced skills.

Examples of independent training include:

1. **Image training**, in which the fighter practices against an imaginary opponent, is good for developing control of advanced skills, fine motor coordination, technical creativity and accurate self-evaluation.

2. **Audio or visual cue training**, in which the fighter responds to predetermined signals or commands, develops quick reflexes.

3. **Fixed target or mirror practice**, using the heavy bag or mirror, develops accuracy.

Training with a Partner

Training with a partner takes place with a limited but active execution of skills according to the varying movements of a partner. Techniques must be performed differently according to the opponent's execution of his techniques and strategy. The competitor must strive for the accurate performance of skills with attentiveness.

Partner training is a direct method of improving the actual competition ability. There are two types of partner training according to the method and goals of training: basic skill drills and strategy training.

1. Basic skill drills

To improve the internal sense of timing, distance and accuracy of techniques, practice with a partner is essential. To develop balance and variety in the offensive arsenal, every skill must be practiced equally with the right and left sides of the body.

Basic skill drills are practiced in pairs. There are **four basic methods of drilling** the competitors: *practice by command* or signals, *free practice* with feinting, *speed and agility practice* and *endurance practice*. All of the drills can be executed in place, moving forward, moving backward or in zigzag patterns. It is best to rotate partners regularly to enhance the competitors' adaptability to different types of opponents. Drills also can be practiced using hand targets for accuracy.

Example A: Hand skill counterattacking drills

The following drills are practiced to develop close distance counterattacking skills:

a. In open stance, the attacker executes rear leg roundhouse kick to the trunk of the defender. The defender uses a rear forearm low block and counters with a lead hand punch to the trunk of the attacker.

b. In closed stance, the attacker executes a rear leg roundhouse kick to the trunk of the defender. The defender uses a lead forearm low block and counters with a rear hand punch to the trunk.

c. In closed stance, the attacker executes rear leg roundhouse kick to the face of the defender. The defender uses a lead arm outside high section block and counters with a rear hand punch to the trunk.

Example B: Kicking counterattack drills

The following drills are practiced to develop middle distance counterattacking skills:

a. In closed stance, the attacker executes rear leg roundhouse kick to the trunk of the defender. The defender counters with an in-place rear leg roundhouse kick to the trunk.

b. In closed stance, the attacker executes rear leg axe kick to the trunk of the defender. The defender counters with an in-place rear leg roundhouse kick to the trunk.

c. In open stance, the attacker executes rear leg roundhouse kick to the trunk of the defender. The defender counters with an in-place back kick to the trunk.

d. In closed stance, the attacker executes rear leg spin whip kick to the face of the defender. The defender counters with a lead leg roundhouse kick to the trunk.

e. In closed stance, the attacker executes rear leg back kick to the trunk of the defender. The defender counters with a back slide, rear leg roundhouse kick to the trunk.

Example C: Footwork counterattacking drills

The following chart lists sample drills to be practiced with a partner in basic training to develop general attacking and counterattacking skills. *Attacker* indicates the actions of the attacking partner and *Defender* indicates the response of the counterattacking partner. *Footwork* indicates the footwork to be executed by the defender before kicking.

Attacker	Defender	Footwork (defender)
back kick	roundhouse kick	backward diagonal step
pushing kick	back kick	"
roundhouse	spin whip kick	"
side kick	whip kick	"
front kick	side kick	"
	front kick	"
axe kick	roundhouse kick	lead foot draw
spin whip	whip kick	forward step
back kick	pushing kick	backward step
push kick	side kick	lead foot draw
	back kick	lead foot draw

The attacker executes a axe kick. The defender counters with a back kick.

Example D: Combined Counterattacking skills **

Attack	Stance	Counter	Footwork	Hand/Foot
Round-	open	back kick	side step	rear
house	"	punch	"	lead
kick	closed	axe kick	"	rear
	"	spin whip	"	"
	"	roundhouse	"	"
	"	whip kick	"	"
Back	both	roundhouse	side step	rear
Kick	"	axe kick	"	"
Axe	both	roundhouse	side step	rear
Kick	closed	"	back step	"
	closed	"	draw	rear
Spin	closed	roundhouse	side step	rear
Whip	"	"	turn back	lead
Whip	open	roundhouse	back step	rear
Kick	closed	back kick	"	"
Punch	open	back kick	in place rear	
	"	spin whip	"	"

** *All attacking skills are executed with the rear leg or hand.*

2. Strategic Skill Drills

Strategic skill drills are professional training methods to perfect necessary skills through consistent repetitive training. Strategic thinking, timing, adaptability, and the ability to execute advanced skills are the key components in this training. There are *four types of strategic skill drills*:

    a. training without protection gear
    b. training with protection gear
    c. training with supplementary equipment (targets)
    d. individual special skill training using a heavy bag

Types of strategic training according to fighting stance:

1. Closed stance

    a. Kicking Attacks

- front leg roundhouse kick
- front leg axe kick
- triple alternating roundhouse kick
- jumping turn kick
- back kick
- front leg side step, front leg roundhouse kick
- front leg side step, front leg out-to-in axe kick
- double roundhouse kick
- in place switch stance, rear leg roundhouse kick
- jumping back kick
- front leg feint, front leg roundhouse kick to face
- rear leg feint, front leg jumping axe kick
- front leg roundhouse kick, double roundhouse kick
- front leg feint, rear leg roundhouse kick
- front leg feint, rear leg axe kick
- front leg feint, jumping turn kick
- front leg feint, back kick

b. Kicking Counterattacks

Attack:	front leg roundhouse kick
Counter:	• slide back, front leg roundhouse kick
	• jumping back kick
	• step back, double roundhouse kick
	• slide back, double roundhouse kick
	• front leg draw, roundhouse kick to face
	• spin whip kick

Attack:	rear leg roundhouse kick to face
Counter:	• diagonal side step, rear leg roundhouse
	• front leg draw, front leg short axe kick
	• front leg draw, simultaneous rear leg jumping roundhouse kick
	• slide back, rear leg short axe kick

Attack:	rear leg axe kick
Counter:	• diagonal side step, rear leg roundhouse kick

Attack:	front leg jumping axe kick
Counter:	• rear leg step back, front leg roundhouse
	• in place front leg roundhouse kick
	• jumping back kick
	• spin ship kick
	• slide back, front leg roundhouse kick

Attack:	jumping turn kick
Counter:	• back kick
	• spin whip
	• front leg draw, front leg axe kick
	• rear leg roundhouse kick
	• slide back, double roundhouse kick

Attack:	aggressive footwork by opponent
Counter:	• front leg short axe kick
	• short slide back, back kick

	• short slide back, rear leg roundhouse kick
Attack:	rear leg roundhouse kick (when you switch stance)
Counter:	• slide back, rear leg roundhouse kick
	• slide back, double roundhouse kick
	• back kick
	• spin whip kick

2. Open stance

a. Kicking Attacks

- rear leg roundhouse kick
- rear leg axe kick
- rear leg roundhouse, withdraw, rear leg roundhouse
- step in, back kick
- double roundhouse kick

b. Kicking Counterattacks

Attack:	back foot roundhouse kick
Counter:	• jumping back kick
	• spin whip kick
	• slide back, rear leg roundhouse kick
	• slide back, double roundhouse kick

Attack:	rear foot axe kick
Counter:	• slide back, front leg roundhouse kick
	• back kick
	• jumping back kick
	• spin whip kick

| *Attack:* | double roundhouse kick |
| *Counter:* | • using footwork, block and attack |

In general, taekwondo competition takes place in closed stance or open stance. However, the actual situation in competition varies according to the opponent's footwork, techniques or deceptive strategy. Complex technical strategy requires direct experience of competition and adequate training to be able to adjust to the varying situations that arise in each match. The current trend in taekwondo competition is a preference for   launching initiative attacks using the front leg and using safe attacks from closed stance by cutting off the opponent's opportunity to score.

Supplementary Training Methods

There is a variety of equipment that can be used to supplement taekwondo training including the heavy bag, forearm shield, weight jacket, wrist weights, and bicycle inner tubes. The most common items are the target, kicking/punching mitt and jump rope.

1. Target and kicking/punching mitt

The purpose of using the hand held target and mitt for training is to improve accuracy, agility, reflexes and power. Every technique must be performed with full focus and maximum reflexive speed. The competitor should attempt to simulate a realistic attacking kick or punch with every repetition. According to the distance to the target, the competitor must also execute the necessary footwork preceding the attack.

During target training, the types of stances, positions, distance and attacks should be varied regularly for a comprehensive workout. To improve coordination, begin with light and simple techniques and build up to more complex and powerful attacks. It is important to practice both left and right sides equally at each training session.

The target holder should stand in walking stance or modified side stance. The target should be held tightly with the elbow slightly bent. It is the responsibility of the target holder to vary the height, angle, distance and position of the target, so the competitor can practice as many skills as possible. When the competitor begins to tire and concentration wanes, target practice should be stopped.

Benefits of target/mitt training

Fixed target	Moving target	Reflex target
explosive power strength maximum accuracy	agility distance control footwork selection	coordination timing speed

The target holder can use one or two targets at varied heights and angles.

2. Jump rope

Jumping rope is economical because it can be done anywhere, at any time, with minimal cost. It is an excellent method for improving cardiovascular capacity, rhythm, lower body power, balance, timing and flexibility. There are two common ways of jumping rope to achieve these benefits:

a. **six one minute round**s with a one minute break between rounds, varying the speed of jumping throughout

b. **three two minute rounds** with a two minute break between rounds, maintaining maximum speed throughout

When jumping rope, keep the upper body, especially the spine, erect and look straight ahead. Relax the shoulder and arms and keep the upper arms and elbows close to the body. Keep the wrists at waist height and use only the circular motion of the wrists to rotate the rope. Bend the knees slightly to increase the elasticity of movements and jump on the balls of the feet. Jumping can be done on both feet simultaneously or alternating feet, with the rope rotating forward, backward or cross handed.

Training System

The following system provides a ready made framework for developing sparring skills in an intensive, interval training format. Each of the skills is performed in a predetermined pattern while aiming for maximum speed and accuracy of execution. For realism, competitors wear full protection gear and attack and defend in the full contact style of competitive sparring.

To make this training successful, the coach should give a brief explanation and demonstration of the skills. The competitors then execute the techniques according to the coach's signals. Once the basics of these drills are mastered, application and variations can be easily developed and applied in free sparring.

The following patterns should be used:

a. **1:1** (single attack vs. single counter)

Example: From open stance, the attacker executes a rear leg roundhouse kick. The defender counters with a rear leg in-place back kick.

b. **2:1** (double attack vs. single counter)

Example: From closed stance, the attacker executes a rear leg back kick, followed by roundhouse kick. The defender counters with a back step and rear leg axe kick.

c. **1:2** (single attack vs. double counter)

Example: From open stance, the attacker executes a rear leg roundhouse kick. The defender counters with a rear leg back kick and front foot roundhouse kick.

d. **1:1:1** (single attack vs. single counter vs. single recounter)

Example: From open stance, the attacker executes a rear leg roundhouse kick and steps down with his kicking leg in front, changing his stance. The defender counters with a rear leg back kick. The attacker slides back and executes a rear leg roundhouse kick.

e. **2:1:1** (double attack vs. single counter vs. single recounter)

Example: From closed stance, the attacker executes a lead leg roundhouse kick, followed by rear leg roundhouse kick. The defender counters with a back step and rear leg roundhouse kick. The attacker recounters with a rear leg back kick.

f. **1:1:1:1** (single attack vs. single counter vs. single recounter vs. single recounter)

Example: From closed stance, the attacker executes a rear leg roundhouse kick and steps down with his kicking leg in front, changing his stance. The defender counters with a rear leg roundhouse kick and steps down with his kicking leg in front, changing his stance. The attacker recounters with a rear leg roundhouse kick. The defender recounters with a rear leg roundhouse kick.

Competitor Styles

The following list provides tips for competitors of different styles to maximize their strong points.

1. Aggressive competitor
   a. conceal attacking intention
   b. diversify attacking style
   c. attack in combinations with maximum speed
   d. execute each technique accurately
   e. take advantage of attacking/countering opportunities
   f. control the distance by varying your stance

2. Counterattacking competitor
   a. execute diverse initiation techniques
   b. avoid and counterattack with good timing
   c. after the opponent's attack, move close and prepare for counterattacking
   d. the use of front leg is more advantageous
   e. block or avoid, then counterattack

3. Short competitor (against taller opponent)
   a. use footwork and feinting to create a chance to attack
   b. when the opponent attacks, avoid or use an immediate counterattack
   c. use infighting strategy
   d. after an attack, close the distance with the opponent

4. Tall competitor (against shorter opponent)
   a. be aware of the opponent's quick dash or attack
   b. when the opponent attacks, cut the attack with the lead leg kick and then counterattack
   c. use long distance strategy
   d. use footwork and feinting to create a chance to attack

5. Distance competitor

a. break the opponent's stance
b. confuse the opponent's sense of distance
c. before attacking, incline the upper body and dash in
d. use quick, surprise attacks
e. use side step or back step attacks

6. Strategic competitor

a. use effective competition management skills to win with minimum effort
b. occupy the central area of the ring
c. if the opponent positions himself near the boundary line, use a combination attack to push him out
d. know that when the opponent frequently, intentionally goes near the boundary, he is setting up a counterattack
e. when the opponent positions himself in the corner, execute a combination attack or prepare to counter
f. when the referee says "kyesok" after "kallyo," attack immediately

Mandatory Protection Gear

There are six types of protective equipment required in WTF taekwondo competition:

a. trunk protector (momtong hogoo)
b. head protector (mori bohodae)
c. groin guard (satbodae)
d. forearm guard (pal bohodae)
e. shin guard (daree bohodae)
f. women's breast guard (yuja kasom bohodae)

The groin guard, arm guard, shin guard and women's breast protector must be worn under the uniform. All competitors also must wear a WTF approved, V-neck taekwondo uniform.

Forearm guard

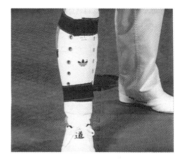

Shin guard

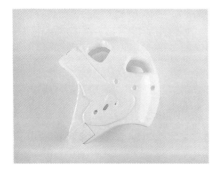

Head gear

Chest guard

Two views of a competitor in full protection gear.

Chapter 6:
Planning and
Implementation

Training is a planned and structured process to create a specific stimulus to the body to improve the fighter's competitive ability. The training must be implemented according to proven principles and methodology.

Goal of Training

The goal of training is to bring out the maximum capacity of the physical condition, technical skill and fighting spirit for the competition.

Content of Training

The training plan must be established based on both long term and short term goals. This is accomplished by creating a daily workout plan based on a comprehensive monthly or yearly plan. To produce maximum results, there are three components that must be carefully considered: intensity of training, duration of training and frequency of training. According to the level of the competitor, the following factors must be included in training:

a. physical strength training
  • fundamental conditioning
  • sport specific conditioning

b. technical training
  • accuracy and power of techniques
  • advanced skills

c. strategic training
  • attack and counterattack
  • individual specialty skills
  • opponent management

d. willpower training
  • meditation
  • mental strength training

e. theoretical training
  • competition rules

Principles of the Training Plan

There are five principles for developing a training plan:

Balance

Balanced training includes the general development of strength, endurance, power, agility, coordination, flexibility, fundamental techniques, and mental toughness.

Comprehensiveness

Comprehensive training means being aware of the task at hand and knowing what method must be used to accomplish it.

Progressiveness

Progressive training means adjusting the quality and quantity of the training load accurately and incrementally while moving toward more complex skills.

Repetition

Repetition training means the continuous practice of skills to instill and enhance natural reflexive responses to competition situations.

Individuality

Individualized training means considering individual condition and specialties and choosing practice skills and intensity accordingly.

Implementation of the Training Plan

Daily training plan

Daily competition training should be done in three 120 minute segments scheduled in the morning, afternoon and evening. This training, intended for elite level competitors, should be organized as follows:

1. **Warm-up** must be done for twenty to thirty minutes to loosen up the joints and improve flexibility.

2. **Core training** lasts eighty to ninety minutes and consists of professional skills and strategies, combination attacks, counterattacks, and supplementary strength and endurance exercises.

3. A **cool down** period is used to relax the muscles and recover the normal mental condition through stretching and meditation for ten minutes.

Yearly training plan

The yearly training plan must specify a time line for achieving specific goals. There are three stages:

1. The first stage is the **preparation period** in which general physical conditioning and basic skills are developed. The division of the training between conditioning and skill training should be fifty percent for each.

2. The second stage is the **intensification period** in which the focus of training shifts toward thirty percent physical conditioning and

seventy percent advanced technical skill development such as the application of kicks, counterattacks, footwork/kicking combinations, speed kicking and agility training.

3. The third stage is the **perfection period** in which the competitor completes the physical conditioning and strives for technical perfection. Training focuses on sixty percent conditioning and forty percent technical training.

Chapter 7:
Progressive
Training Plans

This chapter organizes the skills and drills presented in previous chapters into a progressive curriculum from beginner to expert level training programs.

Beginner Level

Skill level:

Students new to full contact sparring who have a basic understanding of martial arts skills.

Kicks:

1. Roundhouse kick
2. Axe kick
3. Side kick
4. Front kick
5. Punch

Footwork:

1. Forward step
2. Forward slide
3. Backward step
4. Backward slide

Footwork plus kicking:

1. Forward step, roundhouse kick
2. Forward slide, roundhouse kick
3. Forward step, axe kick
4. Forward slide, axe kick

Basic skill drills:

a. In open stance, the attacker executes rear leg roundhouse kick to the trunk of the defender. The defender uses a rear forearm low block and counters with a lead hand punch to the trunk of the attacker.

b. In closed stance, the attacker executes a rear leg roundhouse kick to the trunk of the defender. The defender uses a lead forearm low block and counters with a rear hand punch to the trunk.

c. In closed stance, the attacker executes rear leg roundhouse kick to the face of the defender. The defender uses a lead arm outside high section block and counters with a rear hand punch to the trunk.

Professional skill drills:

1. in-place rear leg roundhouse kick
2. rear leg axe kick

Counterattack drills - closed stance:

A: = attacker, D: = defender

1. A: roundhouse kick, D: side step, rear leg roundhouse kick
2. A: axe kick, D: side step, rear leg roundhouse kick
3. A: axe kick, D: back step, rear leg roundhouse kick

Intermediate Level

Skill level:

Students who have competed the beginner training plan and who are interested in entering local competitions.

Kicks:

1. Punching kick
2. Back kick
3. Jump roundhouse kick
4. Double roundhouse kick

Footwork:

1. Lateral step
2. Lateral slide
3. Turning step

Footwork plus kicking:

1. Forward step, back kick
2. Backward slide, back kick
3. Backward step, roundhouse kick
4. Backward slide, roundhouse kick
5. Lateral step, roundhouse kick
6. Lateral slide, roundhouse kick
7. Lateral step, axe kick
8. Lateral slide, axe kick
9. Turn step, roundhouse kick

Basic skill drills:

a. In closed stance, the attacker executes rear leg roundhouse kick to the trunk of the defender. The defender counters with an in-place rear leg roundhouse kick to the trunk.

b. In closed stance, the attacker executes rear leg axe kick to the trunk of the defender. The defender counters with an in-place rear leg roundhouse kick to the trunk.

c. In open stance, the attacker executes rear leg roundhouse kick to the trunk of the defender. The defender counters with an in-place back kick to the trunk.

Professional skill drills:

1. in-place multiple roundhouse kicks
2. lead foot step in, roundhouse kick
3. quick step, lead leg roundhouse kick
4. in-place double roundhouse kick
5. lead leg pushing kick, rear roundhouse kick
6. in-place switch stance, roundhouse kick
7. in-place roundhouse kick
8. lead foot step in, roundhouse kick
9. in-place back kick
10. lead leg axe kick, slide forward, lead leg axe kick

Counterattack drills - closed stance:

A: = attacker, D: = defender

1. A: roundhouse kick, D: side step, rear leg axe kick
2. A: back kick, D: side step, real leg roundhouse kick
3. A: back kick, D: side step, real leg axe kick
4. A: front leg roundhouse kick, D: slide back, front leg round-house kick
5. A: roundhouse kick, D: slide back, rear leg short axe kick
6. A: axe kick, D: diagonal step, rear leg roundhouse kick
7. A: front leg jump axe kick, D: in-place lead leg roundhouse kick
8. A: front leg jump axe kick, D: slide back front leg roundhouse kick
9. A: jump turn kick, D: rear leg roundhouse kick

Counterattack drills - open stance:

A: = attacker, D: = defender

1. A: roundhouse kick, D: side step, rear hand punch
2. A: back kick, D: side step rear leg roundhouse kick
3. A: back kick, D: side step rear leg axe kick
4. A: axe kick, D: side step rear leg roundhouse kick
5. A: roundhouse kick, D: slide back rear leg roundhouse kick

Advanced Level

Skill level:

Competitors who are experienced (at least one year of competition) in local competition and are ready to move up to more competitive tournaments.

Kicks:

1. Whip kick
2. Spin whip kick
3. Jump axe kick
4. Turn kick
5. Jump turn kick
6. Jump back kick

Footwork:

1. Drawing step

Footwork plus kicking:

1. Forward step, spin whip kick
2. Backward slide, spin whip kick
3. Backward step, spin whip kick
4. Turn step, whip kick
5. Turn step, spin whip kick
6. Draw step, roundhouse kick
7. Draw step, whip kick
8. Draw step, axe kick

Basic skill drills:

a. In closed stance, the attacker executes rear leg spin whip kick to the face of the defender. The defender counters with a lead leg roundhouse kick to the trunk.

b. In closed stance, the attacker executes rear leg back kick to the trunk of the defender. The defender counters with a back slide, rear leg roundhouse kick to the trunk.

Professional skill drills:

1. rear foot step back, double roundhouse kick
2. rear leg roundhouse kick, return to same stance, same leg roundhouse kick
3. lead leg feint, double roundhouse kick
4. lead leg feint, front step in, roundhouse kick
5. front foot draw, roundhouse kick
6. rear hand punch, roundhouse kick
7. lead foot step in, back kick
8. switch stance, back kick
9. lead leg jumping axe kick
10. lead leg feint, simultaneous rear leg jump axe kick
11. in-place spin whip kick
12. lead foot step in, spin whip kick
13. slide back, roundhouse kick
14. in-place lead leg roundhouse kick

Counterattack drills - closed stance:

A: = attacker, D: = defender

1. A: roundhouse kick, D: side step, rear leg whip kick
2. A: spin whip kick, D: side step, rear leg roundhouse kick
3. A: whip kick, D: back step, back kick
4. A: front leg roundhouse kick, D: jump back kick
5. A: roundhouse kick, D: diagonal step rear leg roundhouse kick
6. A: front leg jump axe kick, D: rear leg step back front leg roundhouse kick
7. A: front leg jump axe kick, D: jump back kick
8. A: jump turn kick, D: back kick
9. A: jump turn kick, D: slide back, double roundhouse kick

Counterattack drills - open stance:

A: = attacker, D: = defender

1. A: roundhouse kick, D: side step rear leg back kick
2. A: whip kick, D: back step rear leg roundhouse kick
3. A: punch, D: in-place back kick
4. A: roundhouse kick, D: slide back double roundhouse kick
5. A: axe kick, D: back kick
6. A: axe kick, D: jump back kick

National Level

Skill level:

Black belt competitors who are actively competing at the national and/or international level.

Footwork plus kicking:

1. Front leg side step, front leg roundhouse kick
2. Front leg side step, front leg axe kick
3. Front leg feint, front leg roundhouse kick to head
4. Front leg feint, front leg jump axe kick
5. Front leg roundhouse kick, double roundhouse kick
6. Front leg feint, rear leg roundhouse kick
7. Front leg feint, rear leg axe kick
8. Front leg feint, rear leg jump turn kick
9. Front leg feint, rear leg back kick

Professional skill drills:

1. 360° spin (lead foot pivot), in-place roundhouse kick
2. turn and side step, roundhouse kick
3. switch stance, lead foot draw and roundhouse kick
4. rear foot draw, roundhouse kick
5. switch stance, lead leg roundhouse kick (trunk is fixed)
6. rear foot step in, jumping back kick
7. rear foot step back, lead leg axe kick
8. slide back, spin whip kick
9. in-place jumping spin whip kick
10. step on the opponent's body, jumping spin whip kick
11. rear foot step back, lead leg roundhouse kick to face
12. in-place lead leg axe kick
13. slide back, double roundhouse kick
14. in-place back kick
15. in-place jumping back kick

16. in-place spin whip kick
17. in-place jumping spin whip kick
18. slide back, jumping turn kick

Counterattack drills - closed stance:

A: = attacker, D: = defender

1. A: roundhouse kick, D: side step spin whip kick
2. A: axe kick, D: draw step rear leg roundhouse kick
3. A: spin whip kick, D: turn back step lead leg roundhouse kick
4. A: front leg roundhouse kick, D: step back double roundhouse kick
5. A: front leg roundhouse kick, D: slide back double roundhouse kick
6. A: front leg roundhouse kick, D: front leg draw roundhouse kick to face
7. A: front leg roundhouse kick, D: spin whip kick
8. A: roundhouse kick, D: front leg draw front leg short axe kick
9. A: roundhouse kick, D: front leg draw simultaneous rear leg jump roundhouse kick
10. A: front leg jump axe kick, D: spin whip kick
11. A: jump turn kick, D: spin whip kick
12. A: jump turn kick, D: front leg draw front leg axe kick

Counterattack drills - open stance:

A: = attacker, D: = defender

1. A: punch, D: in-place spin whip kick
2. A: roundhouse kick, D: jump back kick
3. A: roundhouse kick, D: spin whip kick
4. A: axe kick, D: slide back front leg roundhouse kick
5. A: axe kick, D: spin whip kick

Chapter 8:
Kyorugi Psychology

Your feelings about yourself and your opponent are the foremost experience that you encounter before you engage in the kyorugi. Knowing about yourself and your opponent are most important, not only for winning but also for your safety since kyorugi is a contact sport. The sensitivity includes your feelings about the situation that you are in or your intuitive perception that goes beyond explanation. The more accurate your sensitivity about the situation and the opponent is, the better chance for you to win. When you can identify what your opponent is all about through your immediate perception, you are ready to run the game the way you envision. This ability can only come from your direct experience of engaging in every kyorugi practice with the following things in mind:

Empty your Mind

Change is the way of the universe. Winning and loosing are as inseparable as two wheels of a cart. So, you must encompass both sides if you are to be considered a true martial artist. If you are overly trusting that you will win forever, you will one day be caught off guard by more a prepared opponent. So it is essential for you to prepare each day for unexpected moments without being attached to winning or losing. When you are able to transcend this attachment, you are truly free from the uncertainty of the changes. An empty mind will also set you free from fear. Without fear, you can see and judge things clearly.

Be Spontaneous

As a blind man adapts to react to the environment by sound, you must develop your spontaneity. Spontaneity is more than free movement. It is a perfectly calculated maneuver without conscious thought or preparation. It happens without any split between this and that, offense or defense, action or reaction. All come in one. In order to develop it, you must listen to your subconscious. Your subconscious is in tune with the environment. The only hinderance is your conscious thought.

Be Open-minded

Grasp whatever chance you can. Keep your mind open to everything. Your own vulnerability can occasionally be an amazing tactic for luring your opponent into your game plan. Indestructible strengths of the opponent often reveal themselves as cause for self-destruction. So whatever the situation turns into, there always be at least one option for you to utilize. Be boldly open-minded.

Keep the Mental Balance

Always keep your physical balance centered in yourself, because only then will your mind become confident and natural enough to see things as they are in a fight. Your physical posture always affects not only your mental condition but also the effectiveness of your movement. If you lose your physical balance, you are unable to feel right about yourself and most of all you cannot look at your opponent properly from head to toe, from shoulder to shoulder. Your self image and mental focus should not be distorted at any time.

Focus

In the competition, you must allow yourself to only pay attention to what is at hands. Nothing else should disturb you. Set your personal problems aside before you enter the ring. Confine your actions to the fight and learn about things you have never known before. Kyorugi it a tool that can help you grow physically, mentally, emotionally and spiritually. You must discipline yourself in your daily practice that way.

Train with full effort and your ultimate goal in mind at all times. When your mind is focused on your goal, you will feel your inner confidence. When you sense of achieving your goal dominates your mental status, everything else becomes trivial, which helps you believe in yourself and your ability. When you believe in yourself, you can be relaxed enought to do something totally unexpected.

Winning Principles

1. Relax

The muscles function best when they are relaxed. This is very true in any combat sport because when the muscles are tight, you lose the freedom of motion. It is important, therefore, to practice how to relax your muscles in every opportunity in or out of the training place. Relaxation not only helps you conserve the limited supply of your energy but also increases your speed and power.

There are two things for you to do before your match: relaxation of your mind and body. Relaxation here does not mean sleeping. It simply means conditioning your mind and body to the level of optimal naturalness. When your muscles are not too tight, your performance reaches the maximum level. When your mind is in its natural condition, it can fully focus on the moment-by-moment task without being concerned about other things such as fear, family, work, etc. So 40 to 60 minutes prior to the event stretch your body and meditate to set your mind free.

2. Know the Game

Be familiar with rules of taekwondo competition. Master the fundamental skills and fighting strategies. You can observe local, national, or international championships. You can read books or watch video tapes that contain taekwondo competition matches or instructional materials. Ask your instructor or coach about how to prepare yourself for competition. Then know the current trends by watching tournaments and knowing the rules for upcoming events.

3. Know Yourself

Knowing oneself fully is a lifetime mission. It is a simple yet complex process. We humans have so many aspects within ourselves that are beyond complete comprehension. It really perplexes us. But, without knowing yourself, there is no way to measure the opponent. What you know about yourself determines what you want to know about your opponent. What you want to know about your opponent will determine what kind and quality of information you should get. What you know about your opponent will determine what action or reaction you should take. Therefore, before you attempt to spend time to know about your opponent, search deeply within yourself and define the strengths and weaknesses of yourself. Knowing yourself well is the secret to knowing your opponent.

4. Lead the Game

It is very easy to be reactive in competition. When you don't intentionally take action, the opponent will take the leading role. When you become reactive, your opponent may experiment with you in many ways. Even though you are a countering style fighter, you should not passively wait and counterattack. It is too dangerous for you if your opponent is more skilled than you are. Rather you should be proactive in initiating the changes. Use feinting techniques to destroy your opponent's timing. Do footwork to confuse the distance. Make your opponent react to your action. Keep your opponent defensive. When you are proactive, you will gain more confidence in managing the game.

5. Position to Win

After you or your opponent attacks and gets closer, there are two possible situations. It is either you or your opponent who will think the distance is too close for counterattacking. You should never be the one who thinks that way. If you think the distance is too close, you will be stuck there and there is no further attempt but clinching. As soon as it gets close, position yourself using quick footwork to the side angle and hit from there. If the opponent comes in deeply, you should step back and hit. If your opponent runs back, step in deeply and attack. In any circumstance, you should always position yourself for better mobility to be able to execute the next movement. The best position for you to be is where you can attack your opponent in the angle to which he is most vulnerable but you are well covered. When you know this principle, there is no position from which you cannot hit your opponent.

6. Be Direct

The best defense is to attack. The best offense is the most direct attack. Being direct means being most economical and simplistic. The most efficient techniques are often the most fundamental techniques. Keep your techniques as simple as possible but diversify the usage of them as complexly as possible. Whenever there are choices of going directly or indirectly to the target, do not hesitate to think about the choice. Go direct. That way you can conserve your motion and time.

7. Take Initiative

Initiative attacking is superior to defensive tactics. If you only do countering attacks to score, no matter how good you appear to be, in the case of a tie, you will lose against a more aggressive opponent. To ensure victory, you must take the initiative with sharp attacking skills utilizing diverse footwork skills or quick front leg initiative kicks. To be successful in the initiative attacks, you must aim for a variety of the target areas. Do surprise attacks to the target areas where your opponent is not used to getting hit. While both of you are exchanging successive blows in a close fighting situation, whoever changes tactics first might get the winning edge.

By taking initiative action, you can also anticipate the reaction of your opponent. If you give a sign of immediate attacking, your opponent may attack you first out of fear. It is not an obviously physical but psychological attack of you. Your physical initiative attack will cause certain changes in your opponent. The opponent may do an inplace counterattack, step back, move in, or side step out. However he reacts, you will have following opportunities: the chance to attack before he moves, when he moves, and after he moves. Your one initiation can creates three options for you. So don't wait. Take the initiative.

8. Avoid Strength, Strike Weakness

If your opponent is an excellent counterattacker with right leg back and you are repeatedly countered whenever you attempt left leg kicks, you should avoid using your left leg attack. Avoid confronting the strength of your opponent. It is all right to avoid. Change your tactic. Do a fake left leg kick. As soon as he attempts to turn his body for his right leg back kick, throw your right leg roundhouse kick to his right rib cage before his body is fully turned. Avoid strength, but strike his weakness. There is no absolute strength in any technique. Every technique has its own weakness in either space or time.

9. Set-up

A set-up is a more than a fake. It is a tactically calculated risk. The main idea is in utilizing the conditioned response of human instinct. It is a mental device of trapping. Prior to your attempt to set-up your opponent, you should have already identified the fighting style and habits of your opponent fully. An example of a set-up is to attack the trunk section with a roundhouse kick continuously, and when your opponent is very conditioned to the defense of the middle section, you suddenly throw an axe kick straight to his face.

10. Feint

The main purpose of feinting is to deceive the opponent and make him react. His reactions could be 1) blocks, 2) counterattack, 3) back step, 4) forward step, 5) side step, or 6) making unexpected mistakes. Every reaction reveals its own opening which you should be able to grasp in a split second. Feinting should always be followed by an attack.

11. Do Not Change What Works

If your specialty technique works, don't change it. Use the same technique to variable target areas. Some opponents have trouble in fighting against a certain type of fighters or techniques. So as long as your particular technique keeps working, stick to it until the effectiveness starts to fade.

12. Diversify Your Approaches

As soon as your opponent figures out what your tactics are, change to the next plan. If you have been successful in counterattacking with the rear leg roundhouse kick, change to the front leg axe kick to the face the next time. It will shock your opponent. When your opponent hesitates due to the change of tactics, it's time for you to attack aggressively.

13. Take Risks

What you have learned and practiced is what you mainly depend on in the competition. It makes you feel secure. However, if you only cling to what you have learned, you will limit yourself to habitual reactions. You will encounter situations that you have never been in before. Within the boundary of calculated risk, boldly attempt new things that you think will work. That's how new techniques are being developed. New things are discovered from something different. Embrace them.

14. Hit in Motion

When your opponent is in standing in a guarded position, use your footwork and feint him or her into motion. It is not easy to score when the opponent is in a perfect defensive position. Fake the opponent out to move forward or backward. While the opponent is in motion, you will find the opening. If your opponent doesn't move at all, make an aggressive attack and overpower the opponent or change your position to the side and hit him while he changes.

15. Constantly Pressure Your Opponent

When your opponent hesitates, make a strong attack and get in for in-fighting. By decisive attacking you can make your opponent defenseless. By unpredictable tactics, you can have your opponent constantly on guard. As soon as your opponent begins to rest, take a strong initiative and attack deeply. Move in and out in different rhythm. Alternate the speed and targets.

16. Unpredictable Timing

Changing the pace of your motion confuses the sense of timing of your opponent. Set unpredictable patterns for your movements. Combine a technique of normal speed with slow and fast attacks. Feint and move back when he counterattacks. Change your initiative attack to passive waiting tactics. Change your long range fighting into a sudden in-fight. By varying the timing and pace, you can keep your opponent confused.

17. Change the Game

The fundamental strategy is to fight your opponent the way he or she fights if you are confident in what you do. That will convince your opponent that you are better than he or she is, causing the opponent to doubt his or her ability. Once you have the winning momentum, it's time to launch your own fighting plan. When you launch your game plan, don't be afraid of changing your tactics until you find out what works. But never change what works as long as it keeps working. In the mean time, mix what works with what is new, which will keep your opponent on his toes. The benefit of changing is to keep the opponent in constant anticipation. In another words, keep him or her in a defensive position. Then, you will be the one who runs the game.

18. Never Stop Learning

We usually do things according to the ways we learned from early childhood. Often we do things the way we usually do without questioning why. That habitual way of thinking can limit our growth. In competition, if you only do things the way someone taught you, you will do your work in someone else's way. You cannot be yourself. To be truly yourself in either competition or life, you should constantly learn better and different ways of doing things. If you encounter the opponent who has thoroughly studied your fighting style, your chances of winning against him or her get slimmer, so never limit yourself within the boundary of what you know or have learned. Expand your knowledge constantly. Never stop learning about yourself and others.

19. Evaluate Yourself

After competition, whether you won or lost you must sit down and seriously analyze your performance. Never degrade yourself when you have lost. Destroy the destructive habits of your mind. Take defeat as a process of learning. Learn to beat the pain mentally. Be positive.

Do not think of yourself too negatively. After all, you did your best at the time. Focus your efforts more on figuring out why you lost and finding out the solutions that will help you next time. If conventional methods you learned from your teacher did not work out for you, move on. There is no time for outdated thinking. You must progress. If you find negatively habitual techniques, decisively change them or replace them with alternatives. Take a look at the techniques you scored with, the footwork with which you outmaneuvered your opponent, the techniques with which your opponent scored, and the opportunities that you missed. Strive hard to be better. As long as you do not stop being better, you didn't lose yet.

Chapter 9:
Taekwondo Fitness

Physical Condition

Physical condition means the physical capacity that is required to complete a specific task. In taekwondo training, physical condition is measured by strength, endurance and coordination. Strength measures the capacity of the muscular system, endurance measures the capacity of the cardiovascular system and coordination measures the capacity of the nervous system.

Strength and Power

Strength is force that is applied in a static condition. The concept of power includes speed and force. Expressed as an equation: *power = force x speed (speed = distance/velocity)*.

Therefore, power is the capacity for explosive and forceful execution of a movement by the corresponding muscles. To increase power, speed and force must be enhanced by developing the contraction capacity of the muscles. This is especially important in taekwondo competition where skills must be executed with maximum speed and force to score.

There are two types of training to develop these attributes for taekwondo competitors:

1. **Strength training** - Strength training includes weight training for overall conditioning, muscle specific weight training, isometric exercises and resistance training.

2. **Power training** - Power training is done to enhance muscular speed. Power training includes shadow sparring with light weights, bicycle tube training, target drills, stair running, uphill running, vertical leaping and jumping kicking drills.

Sample Strength and Power Exercises

Strength & Power #1

Drop both legs to the right/left

Raise both legs straight up

Drop both legs directly overhead

Strength & Power #2

Beginner: Raise the trunk & legs simultaneously

Advanced: Lift the legs and trunk fully off the ground

Expert: Touch the head to the knees and hold

Strength & Power #3

Alternately lift the legs while keeping the knees straight.

Strength & Power #4

Raise the feet and upper body simultaneously.

Strength & Power #5

Raise the body using the upper arm, shoulder and back muscles.

Strength & Power #6

Beginning in push-up position, alternately twist to the right/left.

Strength & Power #7

Lean forward, stretching the arms out parallel to the ground.

Drop the upper body and reach backwards through the legs.

Speed

Speed is one of the most important physical attributes in taekwondo competition. It is the ability to move the body or part of the body from one point to another in the shortest possible time. There are several different types of speed that taekwondo competitors must develop including:

- the ability to perform the same technique at the same speed repetitively
- the ability to move from one place to another quickly
- the ability to move the arms and legs with maximum speed without regard for accuracy of movement
- the ability to move a specific part of the body quickly

To enhance speed, the competitor must strengthen the ability to integrate the many parts of the body into one explosive unit.

The most efficient method of speed development is interval training in which taekwondo skills are performed realistically and at top speed. Between these intervals of activity, the competitor must rest sufficiently to recover his physical condition and mental concentration. Some of examples of **interval training** for competitors are:

- 25 to 30 meter sprinting
- vertical jumping, touching both knees to the chest
- explosive kicking or footwork drills
- zigzag running
- shuttle run
- jumping rope
- signal training

Agility

Agility means the ability to change direction or body position quickly and proceed with another action. It is closely related to strength, reflexes, speed, power, coordination and flexibility. Agility is determined by the contraction speed of the muscle and the reflexive speed of the nervous system. It is a critical factor in taekwondo skill performance because every offensive and defensive movement requires quick, complex responses. In competition, the competitor must perform multiple actions in response to the opponent's action. For example, when the opponent attacks, the defender must combine the correct avoiding footwork with a suitable counterattack.

Master Sang H. Kim demonstrates why the ability to move the entire body quickly while performing complex skills is essential in taekwondo.

Sample Speed and Agility Exercises

Speed and Agility #1

Stretch and extend the body while maintaining balance.

Speed & Agility #2

From push-up position, explode upward and clap hands.

Speed & Agility #3

Alternately touch the foot of the extended leg to the opposite hand while looking in the opposite direction.

Strength & Agility #4

Lying on the stomach, alternately touch the foot to the opposite hand.

Speed & Agility #5

Bend forward and touch the hand to the ankle, quickly alternate sides.

Speed & Agility #6

Raise the legs and hips and move the legs in a bicycling motion

Speed & Agility #7

Quickly raise the knee to the chest, alternating sides.

Endurance

Endurance is the ability to maintain an activity for a prolonged period. Endurance depends on the ability of the respiratory system to deliver adequate amounts of oxygen through the blood stream. To improve endurance for taekwondo competition, increase the amount and intensity of training. Some examples of endurance training are:

* running 1,000 meters x 3 sets, with a two minute rest between
* running 100 meters x 5 sets, with a one minute rest between
* sparring 3 minutes x 3 sets, with a one minute rest between
* stair running
* pitching (in-place, alternate knee raises)
* target kicking

Flexibility

Flexibility is the elasticity of the muscles and ligaments. It is a fundamental prerequisite for taekwondo competitors. In general, the degree of flexibility is measured by the range of motion of any technique. The greater the range of motion, the more power that can be generated by muscles. In taekwondo training, it is important to develop good flexibility in the shoulders, waist, knees and ankles.

Stretching is critical for enhancing the range of motion, increasing power and reducing injuries. To maintain flexibility, stretching must be done every day without exception. The best time for flexibility training is after warming-up and after the main training period. The minimum stretching routine for competitors is twice a day for at least ten minutes.

Each exercise should be repeated fifteen times in 3 to 5 sets. Each repetition should be held ten to thirty seconds at the point where the muscle feels stretched slightly beyond comfort. The athlete should continue breathing evenly and naturally throughout the stretching exercises. Generally, breathe out when bending the body and breathe in when erecting the body.

Sample Stretching Exercises

Stretching #1

Alternately lean the body gently to the front and back.

Stretching #2

Rotate the upper body in a circle in both directions.

Stretching #3

Alternately raise each knee to the chest and hold.

Stretching #4

Twist the upper body from side to side.

Stretching #5

In horse riding stance, twist the upper body from side to side.

Stretching #6

Place one knee on the ground and lean forward gently.

Stretching #7

Begin from a standing position and have your partner slowly lower your body to the ground. (Advanced practitioners only)

Stretching #8

In side kick position, stretch to the front and side.

Stretching #9

With one foot flat on the floor, extend the other leg to the side.

Stretching #10

With the legs outstretched, twist the trunk from side to side.

Stretching #11

Cross one leg over the other and twist the trunk to the rear.

Stretching #12

With one leg outstretched, pull the other foot to the chest.

Stretching #13

Cross one leg over the other and lean forward to touch the toes.

Stretching #14

With one leg bent
behind, stretch
forward toward
the toes.

Stretching #15

With both legs
outstretched,
reach forward
toward the toes.

Stretching #16

Raise one leg up
toward the chest
while keeping the
other straight.

Stretching #17

Kneeling, spread the knees outward and lower the hips.

Stretching #18

Split the legs and lower the body to the ground.

Stretching #19

Spread the legs out to the side and stretch alternately to the center and both sides. Vary the upper body position for the most effective stretch.

Stretching #20

Raise the upper body and look upward.

Stretching #21

Kneeling, reach forward with the arms.

Coordination

Coordination is the ability to quickly and accurately accomplish a task in a variable situation. Coordination is essential for learning new skills easily and adapting them as necessary. There are six components of coordination:

A. responsiveness
B. analysis
C. extrapolation
D. integration
E. transformation
F. differentiation
G. timing

Responsiveness

Responsiveness is the ability to react quickly and appropriately to expected or unexpected sensory cues. It is directly related to competition performance and is highly dependent on the opponent's movements. To improve coordination, the athlete must use physical reflex training drills like attack/counterattack drills and mental toughness training to enhance concentration.

Analysis

Analysis is the ability to observe and evaluate the opponent's reaction to your strategy. This includes discerning the opponent's skill level, strengths and weaknesses, habits, favorite skills, etc.

Extrapolation

Extrapolation is the ability of the competitor to forecast his or his opponent's technical or strategic behavior based on experience and observation. Through extrapolation, the competitor can feint or setup the opponent and estimate his response.

Integration

Integration is the ability to perform accurately and strategically in the constantly changing situation of the competition arena. This can be accomplished by the coordination of total body movement with the movements of the individual arms and legs. The following are the most important components in kicking techniques:
- footwork
- trunk movement (vertical, horizontal or spinning)
- arm movement to use reaction force
- lower body coordination

Transformation

Transformation is the ability to manipulate physical techniques and strategic considerations to take advantage of an unfavorable situation. Some examples of this are:
- transformation from failing to predict the opponent's attack
- transformation from attacking with the wrong technique
- transformation from being setup by the opponent's feint
- transformation from an unfavorable external environment (poor conditions, unfavorable spectators, etc.)
- transformation from internal emotional turmoil (insecurity, passivity, arrogance, hyperactivity)

Differentiation

Differentiation is the ability to discern a true attack from a feint or setup. Understanding the nature of the opponent's offensive attack allows the fighter to select appropriate counterattacking skills without falling into the opponent's trap. It is also important in developing a keen sense of distance and timing. Differentiation is essential for an accurate and versatile technical performance.

Timing

Timing is the ability to select the best time or speed for performing the proper technique so as to achieve the desired result. It is the most important factor in taekwondo competition for synchronizing the entire body and executing scoring techniques. Timing ability can be measured through reflex time and execution time. It can be improved somewhat through practice and competition experience, but it is generally an innate skill. Some components that enhance timing are flexibility, coordination, strategic thinking, strategic attacking, rhythm, and tempo.

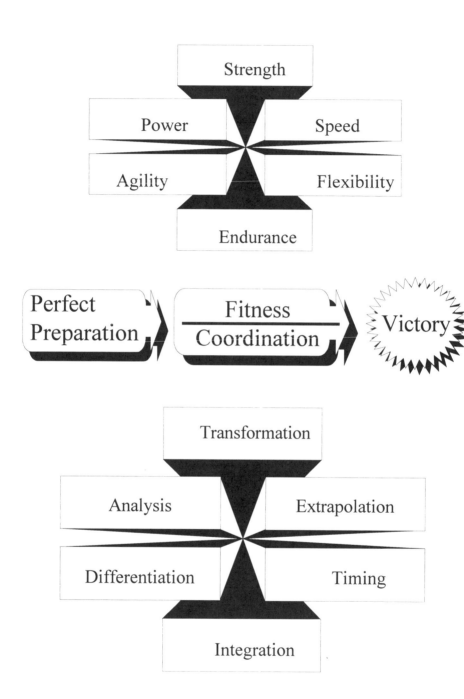

Essential Components of a Taekwondo Athlete

Chapter 10: Coaching Taekwondo

The relationship between the coach and competitor is essential in drawing out the competitor's full potential. There are three basic phases of the coaches duty:

a. Pre-competition

- The coach must assess and prepare for environmental conditions at the competition site.
- The coach must help the competitor finish warming up ten to fifteen minutes before the match.
- The coach must analyze the opponent before the match and provide the competitor with strategic advice.
- The coach must help the competitor to relax and instill confidence in the outcome of the match.

b. During the Competition

- The coach must analyze the overall competition and the opponent's skill level and give advice to the competitor for the next round.
- During the break between rounds, the coach must revitalize the competitor through breathing exercises and reinforcement of the fighting spirit.
- The advice given between rounds must be simple and to the point.
- The coach must refresh the competitor's physical condition by providing water and towels.

c. Post-competition

- The coach must check the physical condition of the competitor for injuries, anxiety or exhaustion.
- The coach must analyze the results of the competition with the competitor.
- The coach must encourage the competitor regardless of the outcome of the match.
- The coach must help the competitor recover his physical condition and restrengthen his mind set.
- The coach must advise the competitor to cool down adequately then shower with warm water for at least 3 minutes and cold water for 1-2 minutes.

Five Qualities of a Coach

1. Comprehension

It is necessary for a coach to comprehend the rules and regulations, techniques, and competition strategies of taekwondo. You must understand the basic elements of the sport. In order to enhance your comprehension of kyorugi, take the following steps:

1) Read the competition rules section of this book.
2) Attend kyorugi clinics and coach clinics.
3) Talk with other, more experienced, coaches.
4) Observe local, national, and international tournaments.
5) Watch Taekwondo championship matches on video tapes.

2. Perspective

Keep your perspective and keep goals in line. The most common objectives as a coach are to enjoy the kyorugi training, to help your students develop their physical and mental skills, and lastly, to compete. So your perspective should involve the priorities you set, and the vision of the future for you and your students. Whether your goal is to have fun, to develop skills, or to win, you must set your priorities in order. Most coaches say that having fun and the development of skills are most important, but when actual competition begins, many coaches emphasize winning. In that moment you should choose between emphasizing your students' development or winning. So before your training season begins, take the following elements into serious consideration:

1) Determine your priorities.
2) Prepare for the situations that may challenge your priorities.
3) Set clear goals for yourself and your students that are consistent with those priorities.
4) Write down how you and your students can best accomplish the goals.
5) Evaluate your goals regularly to make sure that you are on the right track.

3. Character

Character building is one of the most essential goals of taekwondo practice. Kyorugi is not an exception. Whether or not taekwondo practice develops character is your students depends as much as on you as it does on Taekwondo itself. Remember your students always learn by listening to what you say. They learn even more by watching your behavior. You are likely to be a significant role model in the lives of your students. Having good character means modeling appropriate behaviors for taekwondo and life. Therefore what you say and do must match. Be in control before, during, and after all matches and practices. Whenever you make mistakes, acknowledge them openly. Be fair. Do not be biased with regard to gender, ethnic, and other stereotypes. Build your students' ability on their strengths rather than demoralizing them by pinpointing their weaknesses.

4. Affection

Have a genuine concern for the health and welfare of your students. Your understanding of your students and your patience allow each individual to grow from his or her involvement in taekwondo practice. When you care that each student has an enjoyable and successful experience and you encourage them to strive to learn from all their experiences to become a well rounded individuals, your team members will have a strong desire to work with you closely. Know that some learn slower than others. When you can work hard to develop them despite their weakness, then you have the affection necessary to coach your students.

5. Humor

Kyorugi matches and practices always have ups and downs. You or your students might make many mistakes without intention. That's where humor takes a significant role. Humor is having the ability to laugh at yourself and with your students during practices and competitions. Nothing can help balance the morale better than a smile. A sense of humor allows you and your students to enjoy the ups and downs without dwelling on the downs.

Coaching Methodology

Planning is essential to successful teaching and coaching. Effective planning begins well before the competition season. Your planning should include following things:

1) Familiarize yourself with the hosting organization and rules.
2) Examine the availability of facilities, equipment and instructional materials needed for practices and analysis of strategies.
3) Find out what fund-raising you and your students can do to meet your goals.
4) Make arrangements for any travel that will be required to compete.
5) Check to see whether you have adequate paperwork such as liability insurance to cover you when one of your students is injured.
6) Establish your coaching priorities.
7) Designate your assistant coaches, trainers, and other necessary staff, and discuss the philosophy, goal, team rules, and plans for the competition.
8) Hold an orientation session to inform parents of your training philosophy, goals, and approach.

Your choice of activities during the practice season should be based on whether they will help your students develop physical and mental skills, knowledge of rules, and kyorugi strategies. After you have defined the skills and tactics you want your students to learn during the practice, you can plan how to teach them to your students in practices.

Teaching

Be flexible in teaching. If your students are having difficulty in learning a skill, take some extra time until they get the fundamental understanding of it. Remember if your students are unable to perform fundamental skills, they will never execute the more complex techniques you want to teach them. Therefore taking some extra time in the initial learning stage is unavoidable even if that means moving back your schedule. In teaching new skills, follow four steps:

1) Introduce the skill.
2) Demonstrate the skill.
3) Explain the skill.
4) Supervise the student practicing the skill.

At the introduction stage, get the students' attention, name the technique, and explain the importance of the technique in the kyorugi practice.

The demonstration stage is the most important part of teaching taekwondo, especially for those who may never have done anything closely resembling the technique that you are teaching. You need to provide them a picture, not just words. You must show them how the technique is performed. If you are unable to perform the technique correctly, let your assistant or trainer, or one of your students perform the demonstration. The following tips are helpful to make your demonstration successful:

1) Use correct form.
2) Demonstrate the technique several times.
3) Break down each stage of the technique and demonstrate in slow motion if possible.
4) Show the technique at different angles so your students can have a total perspective of the technique.
5) Use both sides of the body equally to demonstrate the technique.

Students learn more effectively when they are given a brief explanation of the technique along with the demonstration. Show them a correct performance of the entire technique and explain its function in competition. Slow down the action and point out its component parts. Have students perform each of the component techniques you have already taught them. After your students have demonstrated their ability to perform the separate parts of the skill in sequence, re-explain the entire skill. When you explain the technique, use simple key words. Relate the technique to previously learned techniques as much as possible. Finally, ask the students whether they understand your explanation.

Practicing

Your teaching job doesn't end when all of your students have demonstrated that they understand how to perform the technique. You should closely observe their practice. Some students need to be physically guided through the movements during their first few practice sessions. Provide positive, corrective feedback. Your feedback will have a great influence on your students' motivation to practice and improve their performance.

Evaluation

At the end of every practice, take a few minutes to review how well the practice attained the goals you have set. It is important your daily goals are consistent with the long term goal. Even if your evaluation is negative, assume a positive attitude and optimism for future practices.

Coaching

After a long period of practice sessions, your students are going to compete. You should have open communication with your students to know precisely what each individual needs to perform best physically, emotionally, and technically. You must check his or her weight regularly to meet the required weight category. You also need to identify the sources of stress and provide alternatives to resolve them. You will be helping your students warm up before the match as well as make sure of his or her registration. Check the list of all the equipments that your students need. Until the competition is completely done, your role as coach is being a:

1) supporter
2) mentor
3) strategic counsellor
4) motivator
5) friend
6) source of knowledge
7) teacher

The most important job for you during the competition is to provide your student with proper coaching tips as the game progresses. Common tips include what to do, what not to do and what to avoid. What to do includes maximum usage of his or her specialties that score points or impact the opponent. What not to do includes habitual movements that create vulnerability or techniques that do not work against the particular fighter. What to avoid includes going straight against opponent's specialities.

Chapter 11: Preparation for Competition

The primary goal of training is preparing for competition. During competition, the competitor deploys skills and tactics learned and reinforced in training. Vigorous training must be geared to develop the full capacity of the competitor for optimum performance. Competition is a part of training as well as the training objective. Professional training contributes to developing the athlete's competitive ability and consistency. Therefor, the level of improvement and the effectiveness of training must be evaluated regularly.

Special Preparation

Special preparation for competition must be started at least four to six weeks before the competition date. The goal and content of the special preparation must be identified and established at the outset.

This identification process includes analyzing the nature of the competition and the types of opponents anticipated. To carry out the competition preparation plan successfully, the following factors must be considered:

1. Weight Control

The best way to control your weight is to balance the amount of food intake and exercise according to your need of gaining or loosing weight. If you loose weight suddenly one or two days before the competition, you may have difficulty in optimizing your full capacity in the competition. It is most ideal to maintain your weight a few pounds of the weight class that you plan to compete in so that you can safely make weight before the match.

2. Energy Management

Taekwondo competition is a match of three rounds of three minutes. If you fight with full power and speed for the whole three rounds, you might be easily exhausted. If not, you may be too tired for the next match. The management of energy becomes more critical when you are getting to the higher levels of competition since it means you will have more fights in one day.

As your experience increases, you will find certain principles that you can depend upon for your judgement according to the type and level of your opponents. The rule of thumb is that the first round is a surveying round unless you know the opponent inside-out, the second is the round for the implementation of your plan to win, the third is to change your tactic or to reinforce what have been working successfully. You must have a few solid techniques that you can fall back on any time. You should aslo be flexible enough to adjust to the fighting style of your opponent without losing your ground to launch your game plan. When you encounter an unexpected style of fighter, don't panic.

Keep the distance. Use a variety of footwork to confuse the opponent and keep yourself safe at the same time. Remember everyone gets tired. Everyone has frustration. So create the opportunity for your opponent to be frustrated and tired. Then you have the momentum to succeed.

3. Confidence of the Competitor

There are only two types of opponents: over-confident or under-confident fighters. Over-confident opponent behave cocky and irritatingly. Under-confident opponent look scared and nervous. If your opponent is over-confident, make a few opportunities for him or her to be frustrated. Over-confident fighters are not good at handling frustrating situations, so keep the opponent frustrated. When you see the signs of frustration, you can draw him into your game plan.

Against under-confident opponent, attack first and read his reaction. You should be careful for your safety because under-confident fighters often do unintentional things out of fear, causing unexpected injuries. Good competitiors are calm and not in a hurry. They have full confidence in their ability and mentally ready to fight against anyone. They compose themselves well with face and shoulders relaxed. Even though they move slowly, you should watch out for a sudden explosion of techniques.

4. Proper Warm-up

Begin your warm-up by finding a quiet place for you to be yourself either alone or with your team members. Shake off hands and legs to reduce the tension in the muscles. Rotate your head to loosen the neck muscles that get easily stiff when you have stress. Breathe deeply ten to twenty times contracting and relaxing the entire muscles of the body. Start stretching your upper and lower body muscles. Then do muscle tension exercises. On the floor, strectch your leg muscles fully with a partner.

When your muscles are warm and supple, begin single kick or combination kick drills to the hand held target or mitt. Each time visualize your fight. Every time you move your body, imagine what kind of reaction your opponent will respond with. Think of all possible scenarios and condition your body and thought to calculated action and reactions. To simplify, fight ten times before you fight.

5. Concentration and Fighting Spirit

When you are not prepared well, you will only be distracted during the match. You must have something to focus. When you have a good plan and preparation, you will feel strong at heart. When you have the feeling that you are completely ready, you are on the way to achieve your goal. The only thing you should be more prepared is that you should not be overly attached to your own feeling itself. If you do, you will have difficulty in handling yourself when the tide comes against you.

Therefore, get real. The reality is that you fight your own game against your opponent's game. He will try to hit you as you do to hit him. There will be serious conflicts that you have to go through. Believe in what you can and should do but be free enough to change your methods of getting what you want without blinding yourself from what your opponent tries to do. When you understand this, you can now stick to your plan and let it fully unfold. Your fighting spirit is the energy that will drive the engine which consists of your physical fitness, technique, and strategy. If all components are equal, the one who has better fighting spirit will be the one who wins.

Competition Observation

Competition observation is a method to enhance the effectiveness of the competitive ability. Therefore the data collected must be accurate and statistical. There are three fundamental ways of observing the competition: recording freely on paper, use of an objective form to record observations, and video taping. During the observation, the following things must be measured: the competitor's ability and capacity, the competitor's attitude, and competition management. Based on these observations, the competitor and opponent can be evaluated as follows:

a. **Competitor**
- analysis and correction of weaknesses and mistakes
- feedback and enhancements of skill level

b. **Opponent**
- prompt information analysis as the situation varies
- analysis of the opponent's weaknesses and errors

Mental Training

Mental training is the most popular method to enhance the competitive ability in every sport in the world today. It has the potential to enhance physical ability by visualizing the execution of skills. Mental training must be based on the experience and observations of the competitor.

The following **factors** must be considered before any mental training method is applied:

a. Visualization requires abstract thought processes to conceive how the skill should be performed.
b. Actual practice must be considered in mental training.

c. Slow movements are good for image training.

d. The combination of physical training and mental training brings results that last longer than physical training alone.

The **benefits** of mental training are as follows:

a. Mental training shortens the learning period of a skill.

b. Abstract thinking enhances consistency of movement.

c. Mental training improves speed.

d. Mental training reduces injuries.

e. Mental training is an excellent supplement during the warming-up period.

f. Mental training is good for reducing errors/upgrading skills.

g. Mental training improves strategic skills like footwork, counterattacking, etc.

h. In competition, mental training helps performance.

Meditation

Meditation has been known as one of the best mental training methods in martial arts tradition for centuries. It calms the energy level in the body, enhances circulation, improves confidence and strengthens concentration. In taekwondo competition, the competitor must execute accurate techniques with maximum power in constantly changing situations, therefore mental calmness and concentration is absolutely necessary to attain victory.

Meditation can be done sitting with the legs crossed in front of the body and the back straight. Attention should be focused on the danjun, the central area of the body believed to be a well spring of energy located approximately two inches below the navel, and the body should be relaxed. The nose and navel should be aligned on a vertical line. Each breath should be deep, calm and long. Visualize a word or phrase to focus the attention.

Chapter 12:
Sports Medicine

Nutrition

Nutrition is the most important aspect in the management of athletes. Nutrition directly affects the training process and results as well as the ability to compete and recover quickly from competition. Good nutrition can be achieved through daily diet management, including the regulated intake of carbohydrates, fats, protein, vitamins, minerals and water.

Carbohydrates can be obtained through grains, potatoes, pasta, and rice. Carbohydrates enhance endurance because they are digested and absorbed by the body quickly (in about ninety minutes) to provide necessary energy. Carbohydrates should make up sixty percent of the daily diet.

Fat can be obtained through butter, nuts, eggs, and fish. Fat should not make up more than thirty percent of the total daily diet. Fat is a direct energy source like carbohydrates. During intense training, carbohydrates are the main energy source, but in less intense endurance training, fat is the main energy source.

Protein can be obtained through milk, butter, cheese, fish and meat. Protein has fewer calories than fat, but breaks down more slowly in the body (in about four to five hours), making it a long term source of energy.

The average male taekwondo competitor needs 3,500 or more calories depending on the intensity of daily training. However, care should be taken in the meal scheduling to avoid fatigue that follows immediately after meals, especially on days of competition or intense training. On the day of competition, the competitor should eat a high carbohydrate, low protein meal two to three hours before the scheduled match. After intense training or   competition, the competitor must eat a high carbohydrate meal to recover the expended energy.

A **sample meal schedule** for competitors:

1. Breakfast	25% of daily intake
2. Snack	10 % of daily intake
3. Lunch	30% of daily intake
4. Snack	10% of daily intake
5. Dinner	25% of daily intake

Tips for eating on the day of competition:

1. Eat a light meal two to three hours before the match
2. During competition, avoid mineral water and sugar based sports drinks. Drink only enough natural water to wet the mouth between matches.
3. Eat lunch one hour after the last match and at least two hours before the next match. If the lunch break is too short, eat bread or fruit as a supplement.

Weight Control

Kyorugi is a competition based on weight classes. The taekwondo competitor should be conscious of his or her optimum weight. Maintaining an ideal weight for his or her physical condition is critical for top performance. The amount of calorie intake during the training period varies according to age, gender, training intensity and duration.

Here are some tips for **daily weight management**:
1. Maintain the optimal weight on a daily basis
2. Use a sauna to sweat off excess water weight
3. Obtain medical advice regarding diet and weight loss
4. Measure and record weight regularly
5. Sweat regularly in daily training

The taekwondo competitor generally wants to compete in the lowest weight division in which he can maintain his physical condition. When the competitor reaches a good weight, he should observe the following cautions to **prevent harmful side effects**:

1. Weight reduction should not exceed more than eight percent of the normal body weight.
2. To reduce weight, the competitor should not sacrifice good nutrition. Eat low calorie but nutritious foods.
3. Adjust the amount of calories carefully during intense training periods.
4. Drink at least one liter of water daily.
5. Take in vitamins and minerals through fruits and vegetables.
6. Do not use drugs or other artificial means to lose weight.

The above advice is for adults only. Children should never attempt to lose weight solely for the purpose of competition.

Massage

Massage is very important for competitors. It helps the body to recover from the physical and mental exhaustion of competition as well as stimulate the muscular and nervous systems. Massage can be used during training, and before, after and during competition. Self massage can be helpful, however massage by a trained professional is much more effective.

To perform sports massage, use the finger tips to press points along the nervous system and blood vessels, stroke the length of the muscles or use the palm to press and shake the muscles in a circular motion. Light massage is safer for athletes than deep massage.

There are three stages of massage. The first stage is to pour massage oil or alcohol on the palm of the hand. The second step is to start massaging the specific part of the muscle with the palm. Gradually intensify the pressure. The final stage is to shake the muscle gently and relax. Avoid massaging injured parts of the body. Spend five to ten minutes for each specific area, and thirty to forty-five minutes for the entire massage.

Types of massage

1. **Post-training massage**. Post-training massage is used to promote circulation and to relax the muscles used in training to speed recovery. The best type of post-training massage is deep massage.

2. **Pre-competition massage**. Pre-competition massage is used as part of the warm-up to enhance the circulation and prevent cramps. It should be a light, gentle massage.

3. **Between round massage**. Light massage between rounds should be used to reduce nervousness, speed recovery and prevent

injuries. For example, the coach can have the competitor sit while the coach holds his ankles and shakes his legs slightly. He also can rub the stomach of the competitor lightly or massage the neck and shoulders to reduce tension.

4. **Post-competition massage**. Post-competition massage is used to recover from the fatigue of competition. The massage should be moderate and not painful.

Injuries

Taekwondo is a contact combat sport in which the competitor is always open to the risk of injury. The most frequent injuries are to the toes, instep, knees, hips and arms. The **major causes of injuries** in taekwondo competition are:

1. Technically unprepared competitors
2. Technically mismatched opponents
3. Overconfidence
4. Overanxiety
5. Inexperience
6. Inadequate equipment/facilities

Tips to prevent injuries:

1. Thorough warm-up
2. Maximum concentration during training/competition
3. Follow the directions of the coach and trainer
4. Proper selection and utilization of safety gear
5. Follow the competition rules
6. A medical advisor should always be present during training and competition.

First aid tips for competition:

1. Carefully observe the injured competitor.
2. If the injury is serious, protect and immobilize the injured part.
3. Avoid moving or touching the injured part.
4. Use RICE: Rest, Ice, Compression, Elevation.
5. Respond promptly and calmly.

Equipment necessary for a competitor's **first aid kit:**

1. Cool spray
2. Adhesive bandages and gauze
3. Antibacterial cream or ointment
4. Massage oil or liniment
5. Scissors
6. Tweezer
7. Sling or immobilizing bandage
8. Disposable rubber gloves

Fatigue

Fatigue is a phenomenon where lactic acid builds up in the body causing the competitor to feel lethargic and decreasing physical capacity. All sports related fatigue comes from the overexertion of the major muscle groups and the cardiovascular system.

The effects of fatigue include decrease in physical capacity, decrease in judgmental ability, increased risk of injury, increased reflex time and decrease in speed

After training, the competitor must have adequate rest and take a hot shower to increase circulation. Post-training massage, adequate sleep and good nutrition are also important.

Chapter 13:
For Instructors

Now that taekwondo is an Olympic sport, the demand for knowledgeable taekwondo instructors and coaches will be greater than ever. However, few taekwondo practitioners have exposure to and experience with training for taekwondo competition at its highest levels. This book makes the training techniques and drills used by international competitors in Korea and abroad available to competitors of every level.

This means that now, regardless of your competition experience, you can train your students the same way that top competitors worldwide are training. However, just reading *Taekwondo Kyorugi* is not enough to effectively prepare your competitors. You must be able to organize a systematic and progressive training plan from the beginner stages. Before you begin planning specific training plans, there are a few general guidelines that must be followed for sparring training: balance, comprehensiveness, progressiveness, repetition and individuality.

Balance

Balanced training encompasses the development of strength, endurance, power, agility, coordination, flexibility, fundamental techniques and mental toughness. Many competitors want to concentrate on advanced skill drills and sparring without giving due attention to the necessities of fitness and conditioning. In standard length taekwondo matches, the competitor must be able to fully concentrate and perform throughout the entire nine minutes. When you factor in the mental and physical stress of full contact blows, the average competitor does not have the innate ability to give one hundred percent for the full three rounds. Through daily physical and mental conditioning, psychological and physiological endurance must be developed.

It is also essential to practice fundamental skills in every training session. Although fancy, complex techniques are more fun to practice, fundamentals win matches. When competitors are evenly matched, the fighter with the better conditioning and sound fundamentals will triumph. As a coach, you must instill discipline in your competitors to allow them to pursue a balanced training plan.

Comprehensiveness

Comprehensiveness means being aware of the task at hand and knowing what is necessary to accomplish it. Each competitor must understand why he is training and what is expected of him. He must know how to apply the skills he is practicing and he must have the strategy necessary to implement the techniques he has learned. If you cram your competitors full of fancy skills without arming them with the knowledge of how to implement them, they will look good in practice but collapse under pressure. As a responsible coach, you should provide each competitor with appropriate technical knowledge as well as the ability to apply it in competition.

Progressiveness

Progressiveness means adjusting the quality and quantity of the training load accurately and incrementally while moving toward more complex skills. In designing a long term training plan, progressiveness is essential in keeping competitors challenged, preventing injuries, developing fundamentally sound skills and preventing burnout.

The training plans in this guide provide you with a model of a progressive system. Progressiveness is what makes training fun and fulfilling for the competitor. It is what provides a sense of accomplishment and improvement.

Repetition

Repetition means the continuous practice of skills to instill and enhance natural reflexive responses to complex situations. Repetition is the essential complement to progressiveness. One without the other will cause the competitor to plateau early in the training period. A lockstep process of progressive training tempered by the repetition of basic, and later advanced, skills creates a fighter who can apply skills with little conscious thought, a reflexive fighter who can respond instantly to any situation.

Individuality

Individualized training means considering individual conditions and specialties and choosing practice skills and intensity accordingly. Not everyone will respond the same way to the same training plan. Allowances must be made to help competitors develop individual specialties based on their body type, physical abilities, psychological temperament and preferences. You cannot create a team of cookie cutter competitors, each exactly like the next. Even though everyone follows the same basic training program, each fighter should be encouraged to develop what comes naturally.

Instructor Fitness

As an instructor and coach, your competitors look to you as an example. They will imitate techniques as you demonstrate them and your explanation will be their guide in applying their skills in competition. To improve your competitors' skills, you have to continue to improve yourself in two areas: your physical ability to demonstrate skills and your knowledge and understanding of the latest sparring strategies.

Creating Your Training Plan

As an instructor it is important to continue your personal skill development, but as a coach, it is essential. You must be able to accurately demonstrate the execution and application of skills for your competitors to model. You must also be able to challenge your competitors to new skill levels by inspiring and motivating them with your own technical proficiency. Simply staying one step ahead of your competitors in the weekly training plan is not enough. You must have your own training schedule that allows you to explore new skills and adapt old skills regularly.

Through your own practice, you can experiment with drills and techniques to see what works and what doesn't, what is suited to your competitors and what is not, what can be adapted and what cannot. You will also find many new ideas and develop skills that are unique to your school. Innovation can give your school an edge in competition by giving your competitors skills that are unique and unexpected.

Dojang Practice Methods

There are many methods of practicing the required drills and skills for competitors at each level. The following sections will give you an overview of how to conduct each type of practice and at what level the methods should be used

Demonstration and practice

Before practicing a new skill, the student must see it demonstrated and explained by you so he or she has a mental and physical model to follow. To introduce a new skill for beginner and intermediate students, first explain the purpose of the skill and how it is used. Then demonstrate the skill in the air, with a target and/or against a partner.

Once the students have a visual concept of the skill, they can begin practicing it slowly on their own or at your direction. For simple skills, allow everyone to practice at their own pace while you correct them individually. For complex skills, break the techniques into steps and guide the students as a group before they practice on their own. At this stage, all practice should be solo. Some students may find it helpful to use the wall or stretching bar as a support. A mirror is also helpful for monitoring the accuracy of each student's movement versus your model movement.

Introducing new skills to advanced students can be less structured. Advanced students already understand the methods of individual practice and can begin solo practice after seeing a movement a few times. You can then work with each individual while they try out the movement on their own. Advanced students will show more variation in learning new skills based on their personal style of training. As an instructor, you must understand their style and help them adapt the new skill to their own best way of using it.

Line Drills

Once the students have a general grasp of the new movement or group of movements, they will be anxious to try them out in a more exciting scenario. Before moving into any kind of contact drill, let them practice the new skill while moving across the floor in a line drill. Make three to five lines of students. The first students in each line begin moving across the floor together executing the skill continuously while alternating legs. After they execute several repetitions, the next group begins. As each group reaches the other side of the room, they return to the end of their line and prepare to begin again.

This drill is especially useful for skills that combine footwork and kicking since the students can get a good feel for the momentum of the techniques. Line drills can used for forward movement, lateral movement and backward movement by varying the starting position of the lines. As the students improve, allowing shorter intervals between groups will cause each group to push the group in front of them to move faster.

When the students have a good repertoire of skills, you can introduce free combination practice, allowing them to cross the floor using rapid fire combinations of movements of their choosing. This drill is good for developing coordination, speed, balance, strategic thinking and total body awareness in intermediate and advanced competitors.

Static Target Drills

Once the student can model a new skill with satisfactory accuracy, he or she can begin practicing it on targets or mitts. It is important that the skill be satisfactory before target practice begins, because students tend to focus on power and speed and forget about technique during target practice. If the technique is already well formed, it can only be enhanced by power and speed. If it is incorrect, it will be imprinted in the students' mind incorrectly through the multiple repetitions of target drills. Incorrect skills executed with seed and power invariably cause injuries, either immediately or over time.

Static target drills can be practiced with partners or as a group. Partner practice involves one person holding the target while the other practices the skill. To provide a challenging workout for both partners, one person should execute the skill ten to twenty times on each side (right and left) then the other person does the same. For beginners ten repetitions is enough. For more experience students, twenty or more repetitions are necessary to create an anaerobic challenge.

Group practice is conducted by forming two teams. One team forms a straight or staggered line holding the targets. The other team moves down the line, one at a time, executing the predesignated technique at each target. After a set period of practice, the teams switch position. This drill is for advanced practitioners. It requires a good coordination and accurate execution of techniques.

Moving Target Drills

Moving target drills use the same skills as static target drills but are conducted with one partner moving across the floor and the other pursing the target and continuously executing techniques. When the pair reaches the end of the floor, they change roles and move back across the floor in the other direction. The coach or instructor can designate skills at various intervals and the competitors should move back and forth across the floor without stopping. This drill is an excellent agility and endurance builder for advanced students.

Partner Drills

Before beginning partners drills, the students must demonstrate control and accuracy of movement to ensure that they do not injure their partners. In partner drills, two students face each other, as in sparring, and practice predesignated sets of attack and defense movements. Partner drills can be practiced with no contact for beginners and light contact with gear for more advanced students. Partner drills are rarely conducted with full contact to prevent unnecessary injury and allow the students to experiment without fear of pain. Partner drills can be conducted as either static or moving, using the same guidelines as in target drills.

Bag Drills

The heavy bag is used by advanced students to develop power and attacking speed. Heavy bag training is suitable for developing linear skills such as roundhouse kick, pushing kick, back kick, turn kick and punching. To prevent knee injuries, it is inadvisable to practice whip kick or spin whip on the bag. The heavy bag should be used only to practice skills that have already been perfected in target drills.

Sparring

The final practice method, and the one in which all competitors are most interested, is sparring. Sparring may be conducted as free or limited and with varying degrees of contact. Beginners should be introduced to sparring by beginning with limited, no contact sparring. Limited sparring means that the students are able to use only a few designated skills in the match. For example, after practicing roundhouse kick drills, students can be coached to apply these skills in sparring. Because they are only using roundhouse kick, they will focus on the correct offense and defense for roundhouse kick without being distracted by other concepts.

When competitors reach the intermediate stage, they are ready to be introduced to light contact and later full contact sparring using their entire range of skills. The process of increasing the range of techniques and amount of contact should be progressive but gradual depending on the students comfort and ability level.

When competitors reach the advanced stage, they should be given the opportunity to practice both free sparring and limited sparring.

In limited sparring, advanced students should focus on using complex combinations of footwork with the limited skills they have available, to develop depth in their sparring arsenal.

Kyorugi in Class

A difficult subject for many instructors is the place of kyorugi training in the daily class curriculum. Many people are turning away from kyorugi training as too "sport" oriented or too limited. If kyorugi is taught properly, it is an essential and useful element in the well-rounded martial artist's training plan.

Kyorugi as Self-defense

Most people find it difficult to make the leap from sparring with rules and gear to self-defense. However, full contact taekwondo kyorugi and self-defense have a number of essential elements. Both require:

1. The ability to perform under pressure
2. The ability to adapt quickly to the opponent's actions
3. The ability to continue to defend and attack while hurt
4. The ability to withstand the opponent's blows and respond without anger or panic
5. The ability to think clearly under duress
6. The need for mental and physical endurance
7. The ability to strike with full power and accuracy
8. The ability to move quickly to block/avoid an attack
9. The ability to overcome fear
10. The ability to spot vulnerabilities and exploit them

Surely everything that goes on in the ring is helpful in developing these skills and can lend the experienced kyorugi competitor an advantage in a self-defense situation. When your students say that kyorugi is just a game or they are interested in self-defense, point out the similarities. Many people just never take the time to compare the two.

Kyorugi without Fear

The thought of full contact sparring is frightening to the average individual. If you take the time to introduce the drills in the order outlined in this guidebook, each student can get used to the idea of sparring through simulations and non-contact trials. As they become more confident in their skills, they will see that they can compete on an equal level with other students of their age and experience level. This will give them the courage and confidence to take the next step toward full contact kyorugi.

Of course, not everyone will be able to take all of the steps necessary to overcome their fear of full contact sparring. And some people have physical limitations that prevent them engaging in contact sports. For these people, you must provide an enjoyable and viable option to full contact kyorugi, such as non-contact sparring or target drills. Structure your curriculum so that students are urged to gradually progress through the many levels of skills and drills until they are fully ready to enjoy the mental and physical challenge of kyorugi.

Chapter 14:
Competition Rules

The World Taekwondo Federation
January 1998

Article 1. Purpose

The purpose of the competition Rules is to manage fairly and smoothly all matters pertaining to competitions of all levels to be promoted and/or organized by the WTF, Regional Unions and member National Association, ensuring the application of standardized rules.

Article 2. Application

The Competition Rules shall apply to all the competitions to be promoted and/or organized by the WTF, each Regional Union and member National Association. However, any member National Association wishing to modify some part of the Competition Rules must first gain the approval of the WTF.

Article 3. Competition Area

The Competition Area shall measure 12m x 12m in Metric system and have a flat surface without any obstructing projections.

The Competition Area shall be covered with an elastic mat. However, the competition area may be installed on a platform 0.5m-0.6m high from the base, if necessary, and the outer part of the Boundary Line shall be inclined with a gradient of less than 30 degrees for the safety of the contestants.

1) Demarcation of the Competition Area

1. The 8m x 8m area in the inner part of the Competition Area of 12m x 12m shall be called the Contest Area and the outer part of the Contest Area shall be called the Alert Area.

2. The demarcation of the Contest Area and the Alert Area shall be distinguished by the different colors of the two areas' surface, or indicated by a white line 5cm wide when the entire surface is one color.

3. The demarcating line between the Contest Area and the Alert Area shall be called the Alert Line and the marginal line on the Competition Area shall be called the Boundary Line.

2) Indication of Positions

1. Position of the Referee
The position of the Referee shall be marked at a point 1.5m back from the center point of the Competition Area to the third Boundary Line and designated as the Referee's Mark.

2. Position of the Judges
The position of the 1st judge shall be marked at a point 0.5m outwards from the center of the 1st Boundary Line facing the center point of the Competition Area and the position of the 2nd judge shall be marked 0.5m outwards from the bottom corner of the second Boundary Line facing the center of the Competition Area. The position of the 3rd judge shall be marked at the opposite point of the 4th Boundary Line with the position of the 2nd judge.

3. Position of the Recorder

The position of the Recorder shall be marked at a point 1.5m back from the position of the 1st judge and 3m to the left.

4. Position of the Commission Doctor

The position of the Commission Doctor shall be marked at a point 6m to the right side of the position of the Recorder.

5. Position of the Contestants

Position of the contestants shall be marked at a point 1m to the respective left and right sides from the center point of the competition facing the position of the 1st judge. The right side shall be the Blue Contestant's Mark and the left side shall be the Red Contestant's Mark.

6. Position of the Coaches

The position of the coaches shall be marked at a point 1m away from the center point of Boundary Line of each contestant's side.

7. Position of the Inspection Desk

The position of the Inspection Desk shall be near the entrance of the Competition Area for inspection of the contestant's protective equipment.

Article 4. Contestants

1) Qualification of Contestants

1. Holder of the nationality of the participating team.

2. One recommended by the national Taekwondo association.

3. Holder of Taekwondo Dan certificate issued by the Kukkiwon/WTF and in case of the World Junior Taekwondo Championship, holder of Kukkiwon Poom/Dan certificate aged

between 14 through 17 years based on the year when the championships are held.

2) The Costume for Contestants

1. The contestant shall wear a Taekwondo uniform (Dobok) and Protectors recognized by the WTF.

2. The contestant shall wear the trunk protector, head protector, groin guard, forearm and shin guard before entering the contest area and the groin guard, forearm and shin guards shall be worn inside the Taekwondo uniform, and the contestant shall bring the WTF-approved protectors for personal use.

3) Medical Control

1. The use or administration of drugs or chemical substances described in the IOC doping by-laws is prohibited.

2. The WTF may carry out any medical testing deemed necessary to ascertain if a contestant has committed a breach of this rule, and any winner who refuses to undergo this testing or who proves to have committed such a breach shall be removed from the final standings, and the record shall be transferred to the contestant next in line in the competition standing.

3. The organizing committee shall be liable for arrangements to carry out medical testing.

Article 5. Weight Divisions

1. Weights are divided into male and female divisions.

2. Weight divisions are divided as follows :

	Male Division	**Female Division**
Fin	Not exceeding 54 kg	Not exceeding 47 kg
Fly	Over 54 kg not exceeding 58 kg	Over 47 kg not exceeding 51 kg
Bantam	Over 58 kg not exceeding 62 kg	Over 51 kg not exceeding 55 kg
Feather	Over 62 kg not exceeding 67 kg	Over 55 kg not exceeding 59 kg
Light	Over 67 kg not exceeding 72 kg	Over 59 kg not exceeding 63 kg
Welter	Over 72 kg not exceeding 78 kg	Over 63 kg not exceeding 67 kg
Middle	Over 78 kg not exceeding 84 kg	Over 67 kg not exceeding 72 kg
Heavy	Over 84 kg	Over 72 kg

3. Weight divisions for the Olympic Games are divided as follows:

Male Division	**Female Division**
Not exceeding 58 kg	Not exceeding 49 kg
Over 58 kg not exceeding 68 kg	Over 49 kg not exceeding 57 kg
Over 68 kg not exceeding 80 kg	Over 57 kg not exceeding 67 kg
Over 80 kg	Over 67 kg

4. Weight divisions for the World Junior Championships are divided as follows:

	Male Division	**Female Division**
Fin	Not exceeding 45 kg	Not exceeding 42 kg
Fly	Over 45 kg not exceeding 48 kg	Over 42 kg not exceeding 44 kg
Bantam	Over 48 kg not exceeding 51 kg	Over 44 kg not exceeding 46 kg
Feather	Over 51 kg not exceeding 55 kg	Over 46 kg not exceeding 49 kg
Light	Over 55 kg not exceeding 59 kg	Over 49 kg not exceeding 52 kg
Welter	Over 59 kg not exceeding 63 kg	Over 52 kg not exceeding 55 kg
Light Middle	Over 63 kg not exceeding 68 kg	Over 55 kg not exceeding 59 kg

Middle	Over 68 kg not exceeding 73 kg	Over 59 kg not exceeding 63 kg
Light Heavy	Over 73 kg not exceeding 78 kg	Over 63 kg not exceeding 68 kg
Heavy	Over 78 kg	Over 68 kg

Article 6. Classification and Methods of Competition

1) Competitions are divided as follows:

1. Individual competition shall normally be between contestants in the same weight class. When necessary, adjoining weight classes may be combined to create a single classification.

2. Team Competition - Systems of Competition

(1) Five contestants by weight classification with the following category:

Male Division	**Female Division**
Not exceeding 54 kg	Not exceeding 47 kg
Over 54 kg not exceeding 63 kg	Over 47 kg not exceeding 54 kg
Over 63 kg not exceeding 72 kg	Over 54 kg not exceeding 61 kg
Over 72 kg not exceeding 82 kg	Over 61 kg not exceeding 68 kg
Over 82 kg	Over 68 kg

(2) Eight (8) contestants by weight classification.
(3) Four (4) contestants by weight classification. (Consolidation of the eight weight classifications into four weight categories by combining two adjacent weight classes.)

2) Systems of competition are divided as follows:

1. Single elimination tournament system

2. Round robin system

3. Taekwondo competition of the Olympic Games shall be conducted in individual competition system between contestants.

4. All international-level competitions recognized by the WTF shall be formed with participation of at least 4 countries with no less than 4 contestants in each weight class, and any weight class with less than 4 contestants cannot be recognized in the official results.

Article 7. Duration of the Contest

The duration of the contest shall be three rounds of three minutes with one minute of rest between rounds in male and female divisions, with that of World Junior Championships being three rounds of two minutes with one minute of rest between rounds. However, the duration of the contest may be shortened to three rounds of two minutes with one minute of rest between rounds with the approval of the WTF.

Article 8. Drawing Lots

1) The drawing of lots shall be conducted one day prior to the first competition in the presence of WTF officials and the representatives of the participating nations, and the drawing of lots shall be done from Fin weight up in the English alphabetical order of the official names of the participating nations.

2) Officials shall be designated to draw lots on behalf of the officials of participating nations not present at the drawing.

3) The order of the draw may be changed according to the decision of the Head of Team meeting.

Article 9. Weigh-In

1) Weigh-in of the contestants on the day of the competition shall be completed one hour prior to the competition.

2) During weigh-in, the male contestants shall wear underpants and the female contestants shall wear underpants and brassiere. However, weigh-in may be conducted in the nude in the case that the contestant wishes to do so.

3) Weigh-in shall be made once; however, one more weigh-in is granted within the time limit for official weigh-in to the contestant who did not qualify the first time.

4) So as not to be disqualified during official weigh-in, a scale, the same as the official one, shall be provided at the contestants' place of accommodation or at the arena for preweigh-in.

Article 10. Procedure of the Contest

1) Call for Contestants

The name of the contestants shall be announced three times beginning three minutes prior to the scheduled start of the contest. The contestant who fails to appear in the contest area within one minute after the scheduled start of the competition shall be regarded as withdrawn.

2) Physical and Costume Inspection

After being called, the contestants shall undergo physical and costume inspection at the designated inspection desk by the inspector designated by the WTF, and the contestant shall not show any signs of aversion, and also shall not bear any materials which could cause harm to the other contestant.

3) Entering the Competition Area

After inspection, the contestant shall enter into the waiting position with one coach.

4) Start and End of the Contest

The contest in each round shall begin with the declaration of "Shijak" (Start) by the Referee and shall end with the declaration of "Keuman" (Stop) by the Referee.

5) Procedure Before the Beginning and End of the Contest

1. The contestants shall face each other and make a standing bow at the Referee's command of "Charyeot" (Attention) and "Kyeongrye" (Bow). A standing bow shall be made from the natural standing posture of "Charyeot" be inclining forward at the waist to an angle of more than 30 degrees with the head inclining to an angle of more than 45 degrees and the fists clenched at the sides of the legs.

2. The Referee shall start the contest by commanding "Joonbi" (Ready) and "Shijak" (Start).

3. At the end of the last round, the contestants shall stand at their respective position facing each other and exchange a standing bow at the Referee's command of "Charyeot" and "Kyeongrye," and then wait for the Referee's declaration of the decision in a standing posture.

4. The Referee shall declare the winner by raising his/her own hand to the winner's side.

5. Retirement of the contestants.

6) Contest Procedure in Team Competition

    1. Both teams shall stand facing each other in line in submitted team order towards the first Boundary Line from the contestants' marks.

    2. Procedure before the beginning and after the end of the contest shall be conducted as in Item 5 of this Article.

    3. Both teams shall leave the Contest Area and stand by at the designated area for each contestant's match.

    4. Both teams shall line up in the Contest Area immediately after the end of the final match facing each other.

    5. The Referee shall declare the winning team by raising his/her own hand to the winning team's side.

Article 11. Permitted Techniques and Areas

1) Permitted Techniques

    1. Fist techniques: Delivering techniques by using the front parts of the forefinger and middle finger of the tightly clenched fist.

    2. Foot techniques: Delivering techniques by using the foot below the ankle bone.

2) Permitted Areas

    1. Trunk: Within the limits of the area from a horizontal line at the base of the Acromion down to a horizontal line at the iliac crest, attack by fist and foot techniques are permitted. However, such attacks shall not be made on the part of the back not covered by the trunk protector.

2. Face: This area is the front part of the face on the basis of a coronal line at both ears, and attack by foot technique only is permitted.

Article 12. Valid Points

1) Legal Scoring Area

1. Mid-section of the trunk: The abdomen and both sides of the flank.

2. Face: The permitted parts of the face.

2) Points shall be awarded when permitted techniques are delivered accurately and powerfully to the legal scoring areas of the body. However, when a contestant is knocked down as a result of the opponent's attack on a part of the trunk protector which is not part of a legal scoring area, such technique shall be regarded as a point.

3) Each scoring technique shall earn 1 (plus one) point.

4) Match score shall be the sum of points of the three rounds.

5) Invalidation of points: When the following are committed, the delivered technique will not be scored:

1. Intentionally falling, immediately after delivery of the legitimate technique.

2. Committing an illegal act after delivery of the legitimate technique.

3. Use of any of the prohibited actions.

Article 13. Scoring and Publication

1) Valid points shall be immediately recorded and publicized.

2) In the use of body protectors not equipped with electronics, valid points shall be immediately marked by each judge by using an electronic scoring instrument or judge's scoring sheet.

3) In the use of electronic trunk protectors:

1. Valid points scored on the midsection of the trunk shall be recorded automatically by the transmitter in the electronic trunk protectors.

2. Valid points scored to the face shall be marked by each judge by using the electronic scoring instrument or judge's scoring sheet.

4) In the case of scoring by using the electronic scoring instrument or judge's scoring sheet, valid points shall be the ones recognized by two or more judges.

Article 14. Prohibited Acts

1) Penalties on any prohibited acts shall be called by the Referee.

2) In the case of multiple penalties being committed simultaneously, the heavier penalty shall be declared.

3) Penalties are divided into Kyong-go (warning penalty) and Gam-jeom (deduction penalty).

4) Two Kyong-gos shall be counted as a deduction of one (1) point. However, the last odd Kyong-go shall not be counted in the grand total.

5) A Gam-jeom shall be counted as minus one (-1) point.

6) Prohibited Acts: Kyong-go Penalty:

1. Touching Acts

a. Grabbing the opponent
b. Holding the opponent
c. Pushing the opponent
d. Touching the opponent with the trunk

2. Negative Acts

a. Intentionally crossing the alert line
b. Evading by turning the back to the opponent
c. Intentionally falling down
d. Pretending injury

3. Attacking Acts

a. Butting or attacking with the knee
b. Intentionally attacking the groin
c. Intentionally stamping or kicking any part of the leg or foot
d. Hitting the opponent's face with hands or fist

4. Undesirable Acts

a. Gesturing to indicate scoring or deduction on the part of the contestant or the coach
b. Uttering undesirable remarks or any misconduct on the part of the contestant or the coach
c. Leaving the designated mark on the part of the coach during match

7) Prohibited Acts: Gam-jeom Penalty

1. Touching Acts

a. Throwing the opponent
b. Intentionally throwing the opponent by grappling the
   opponent's attacking foot in the air with the arm

2. Negative Acts

a. Crossing the boundary line
b. Intentionally interfering with the progress of the match

3. Attacking Acts

a. Attacking the fallen opponent
b. Intentionally attacking the back and the back of the head
c. Attacking the opponent's face severely with the hand

4. Undesirable Acts

a. Violent or extreme remarks or behavior on the part of the
   contestant or the coach

8) When a contestant refuses to comply with the Competition
Rules or the Referee's order intentionally, the Referee may declare the
contestant the loser by penalty.

9) When the contestant receives minus three (-3) points, the
Referee shall declare him/her the loser by penalties.

10) Kyong-go and Gam-jeom shall be counted in the total score
of the three rounds.

Article 15. Decision of Superiority

1) In the case of a tie score by deduction of points, the winner shall be the contestant awarded any point or more points through the three rounds.

2) In the case of a tie score other than case 1 above (where both contestants received the same number of points and/or deductions), the winner shall be decided by the Referee based on superiority throughout all three rounds.

3) Decision of superiority shall be based on the initiative shown during the contest.

Article 16. Decisions

1. Win by K.O.
2. Win by Referee stopping the contest (R.S.C.)
3. Win by score or superiority
4. Win by withdrawal
5. Win by disqualification
6. Win by Referee's punitive declaration

Article 17. Knock Down

1) When any part of the body other than the sole of the foot touches the floor due to the force of the opponent's delivered technique.

2) When the contestant is staggered showing no intention or ability to pursue the match.

3) When the Referee judges that the contest cannot continue as the result of any power technique having been delivered.

Article 18. Procedure in the Event of a Knock Down

1) When a contestant is knocked down as the result of the opponent's legitimate attack, the referee shall take the following measures:

1. The Referee shall keep the attacker away from the downed contestant by declaration of "Kalyeo" (Break).

2. The Referee shall count aloud from "Hanah" (One) up to "Yeol" (Ten) at one second intervals towards the downed contestant making hand signals indicating the passage of time.

3. In case the downed contestant stands up during the Referee's count and desires to continue the fight, the Referee shall continue the count up to "Yeodul" (Eight) for recovery of the downed contestant. The Referee shall then determine if the contestant is recovered and, if so, continue the contest by declaration of "Kyesok" (Continue).

4. When a contestant who has been knocked down cannot demonstrate the will to resume the contest by the count of "Yeodul," the Referee shall announce the other contestant the winner by K.O.

5. The count shall be continued even after the end of the round or the expiration of the match time.

6. In case both of the contestants are knocked down, the Referee shall continue counting as long as one of the contestants has not sufficiently recovered.

7. When both of the contestants fail to recover by the count of "Yeol," the winner shall be decided upon the match score before the occurrence of the knock down.

8. When it is judged by the Referee that a contestant is unable to continue, the Referee may decide the winner either without counting

or during the counting.

2) Procedures To Be Followed After the Contest

Any contestant suffering a knock-out as the result of a blow to the head, will not be allowed to compete for the next 30 days.

Before entering a new contest after 30 days, the contestant must be examined by a medical doctor designated by the National Taekwondo Federation, who must certify that the contestant is recovered and able to compete.

Article 19. Procedures for Suspending the Match

1) When a contest is to be stopped due to the injury of one or both of the contestants, the Referee shall take the following measures:

1. The referee shall suspend the contest by declaration of "Kalyeo" and order the Time Keeper to suspend the time keeping by announcing "Kyeshi."

2. The Referee shall allow the contestant to receive first aid within one minute.

3. The contestant who does not demonstrate the will to continue the contest after one minute, even in the case of a slight injury, shall be declared the loser by the Referee.

4. In case resumption of the contest is impossible after one minute, the contestant causing the injury by a prohibited act to be penalized by Gam-jeom shall be declared the loser.

5. In case both of the contestants are knocked down and are

unable to continue the contest after one minute, the winner shall be decided upon points scored before the injuries occurred.

6. When it is judged that the contestant's health is at risk due to losing consciousness of falling in an apparently dangerous condition, the Referee shall suspend the contest immediately and order first aid to be administered. The Referee shall declare as loser, the contestant causing the injury if it is deemed to have resulted from a prohibited act to be penalized by Gam-jeom, or in the case the attack was not deemed to be penalized by Gam-jeom, shall decide the winner on the basis of the score of the match before suspension of the time.

Article 20. Referees and Judges

1) Qualifications

Holders of International Referee Certificate registered by the WTF.

2) Duties

1. Referee

a. The Referee shall have control over the match.

b. The Referee shall declare "Shijak," "Keuman," "Kalyeo," Kyesok," and "Kyeshi," winner and loser, deduction of points, warnings and retiring. All the Referee's declarations shall be made when the results are confirmed.

c. The Referee shall have the right to make decisions independently in accordance with the prescribed rules.

d. The Referee shall not award points.

e. In case of a tied or scoreless match, the decision of superiority shall be made by the Referee after the end of three rounds.

2. Judges

a. The Judges shall mark the valid points immediately.

b. The Judges shall state their opinions forthrightly when requested by the Referee.

3) Responsibility for Judgement

Decisions made by the Referees and Judges shall be conclusive and they shall be responsible to the Board of Arbitration for those decisions.

4) Uniform of the Referees and Judges

1. The Referees and Judges shall wear the uniform designated by the WTF.

2. The Referees and Judges shall not carry or take any materials to the arena which might interfere with the contest.

Article 21. Recorder

The Recorder shall time the contest and periods of time-out, suspension, and shall also record and publicize the awarded points, and/or deduction of points.

Article 22. Assignment of Officials

1) Composition of refereeing officials

1. In the use of non-electronic trunk protectors:
The officials are composed of one Referee and three Judges.

2. In the use of electronic trunk protectors:
The officials are composed of one Referee and two Judges.

2) Assignment of Refereeing Officials

1. The assignment of the Referees and Judges shall be made after the contest schedule is fixed.

2. Referees and Judges with the same nationality as that of either contestant shall not be assigned to such a contest. However, an exception shall be made for the Judges when the number of refereeing officials is insufficient as the case may be.

Article 23. Other Matters Not Specified By the Rules

In the case that any matters not specified in the Rules occur, they shall be dealt with as follows:

1) Matters related to the competition shall be decided through consensus by the refereeing officials of the pertinent contest.

2) Matters which are not related to a specific contest shall be decided by the Executive Council or its proxy.

3) The Organizing Committee shall prepare a video tape recorder at each court for recording and preservation of the match progress.

Article 24. Arbitration

1) Composition of Board of Arbitration

1.Qualifications: Member of Executive Council of WTF or person of sufficient Taekwondo experience recommended by WTF President of Secretary General.

2.Composition: One Chairman and less than six members.

3.Procedure of Appointment: The Chairman and members of the Board of Arbitration will be appointed by the WTF President on the recommendation of the WTF Secretary General.

2) Responsibility

The Board of Arbitration shall make corrections of misjudgments according to their decision regarding protests and take disciplinary action against the officials committing the misjudgment or any illegal behavior and the results of which shall be sent to the Secretariat of the WTF.

3) Procedure of Protest

1. In case there is an objection to a judgement, a delegate must submit an application for reevaluation of decision (protest application) together with the prescribed fee to the Board of Arbitration within 10 minutes after the pertinent contest.

2. Deliberation of reevaluation shall be carried out excluding those members with the same nationality as that of either contestant concerned, and resolution on deliberation shall be made by majority.

3. The members of the Board of Arbitration may summon the refereeing officials for confirmation of events.

4. The resolution made by the Board of Arbitration will be final and no further means of appeal will be applied.

Enacted: May 28, 1973
Revised: October 1, 1977
Revised: February 23, 1982
Revised: October 19, 1983
Revised: June 1, 1986
Revised: October 7, 1989
Revised: October 28, 1991
Revised: August 17, 1993
Revised: November 18, 1997

Referee's Hand Signals

Call for Contestants

1. Clenching the fist with the thumb on the middle finger, and spreading out the forefinger.

2. Stretching out the arm from the chest, "Chung" contestant's mark shall be pointed first with the right forefinger, and next "Hong" contestant's mark with the left forefinger.

Charyut / Kyungrye (attention/bow)

1. Vertically and parallelly raising the palms of both hands with the thumbs on the palms at a height of the eyebrow with the arms outstretched at an angle of 45 degrees from the points of both shoulders, and

2. Giving a verbal order of "Cha-ryut," and then

3. Taking down the hands with the palm down to the front of the stomach, a verbal order of "Kyung-rye" shall be given.

Joon-bi (ready)

1. Outstretching the crooked right arm at an angle of 45 degrees from the point of the right shoulder

2. Vertically raising the palm of the right hand at the height of the ear, and taking a step forward the posture of the left-front-walking ("Wen-ab-goo-bi") shall be taken, and then

3. Taking down the right hand in a knife-hand position to the height of the stomach, a verbal order of "Joon-bee" shall be given.

4. At this point, the left hand lightly clenched shall be straightened down.

Shijak (begin)

1. Taking the posture of "Bum-seo-ki" from the posture of "Joon-bee" by withdrawing the left foot back, both arms shall be outstretched at an angle of 45 degrees from the point of both shoulders, and then

2. With the arms rapidly closing up before the breast, an order of "Shi-jak" shall be given.

Kalyeo / Keoman (break)

Taking a posture of the left walking stance, the right knife-hand shall be rapidly taken down at a height of the stomach giving an order of "Kal-yeo" / "Keo-man."

Kyesok (continue)

Raising the right knife-hand from the posture of "Kal-yeo" at a height of the right ear, the order of "Kye-sok" shall be given.

Winner Declaration

1. When "Chung" is the winner, the Referee shall turn towards "Chung" and raise the right fist to the stomach, and then immediately

stretch the knife-hand up at an angle of 45 degrees declaring "Chung Seung."

2. In case of "Hong," the Referee shall declare "Hong Seung" by using the left knife-hand in the same manner.

3. At this point, the other hand lightly clenched shall be at the side.

Kyeshi (record time)

Straightening down the right hand with the arm bent at an angle of 135 degrees, the Referee shall point the right forefinger at the Recorder's seat.

Shigan (time)

This is demonstrated by making an X mark by crossing both forefingers at a height of the perpendicular furrow of the upper lip.

Counting

The count shall be made from the right thumb by spreading out the fingers of the clenched fist one by one at one second intervals giving a verbal count. When the count reaches "Da-seot" (five) and "Yeol" (ten), the palm shall be turned toward the pertinent contestant.

Kyong-go Penalty

1. Touching Acts

1. Looking at the pertinent contestant in the posture of "Charyut," the Referee shall point the right forefinger at the contestant, and

2. Putting the right palm on the left chest (the right middle finger to reach the left shoulder blade), "Kyong-go" shall be declared.

2. Negative Acts

The motion of two times bumping the fists, leaving an interval of a fist between the two clenched fists, in front of the stomach.

3. Attacking Acts

Vertically raising the left palm up to the height of the shoulder, one time punching with the right fist shall be given on the left palm.

4. Undesirable Acts

The motion of bringing the right forefinger to the lips leaving an interval of 5cm between the lips and the forefinger.

Motion of Kyong-go Declaration

1. The right fist shall be lightly clenched with the forefinger spread out in the posture of "Charyut," and then

2. Pointing the right forefinger at the middle of forehead of the pertinent contestant by spreading out the right arm bent at an interior angle of 135 degrees, giving a verbal indication of "Hong" or "Chung,"

3. And then bringing the right forefinger to the left shoulder,

4. Pointing the right forefinger at the middle of the forehead of the contestant by horizontally spreading out the arm, the Referee shall make the declaration of "Kyong-go."

Motion of Gam-jeom Declaration

All the motions are the same as those of the "Kyong-go" penalty with the exception of the motion of "Gam-jeom" declaration.

1. After pointing at the pertinent contestant in the posture of "Charyut" same as the procedure of "Kyong-go" declaration,

2. Straightly raising the right fist tightly clenched with the forefinger spread out, the Referee shall make a verbal declaration of "Gam-jeom."

Appendix A:
Taekwondo Competition
Terminology

A

apchook	ball of foot

B

badah chagi	counter kicking
bal	foot
balbadak	sole of foot
baldung	instep
bal jitgi	footwork
banguh	defense
bankyug	counterattack
baro	return to ready stance
bikyu jitgi	side step
boosang	injury
booshim	corner judge

C

chagi	kick
chajumpyo	judging paper
charyut	attention
chegup	weight division
chung	blue
chung sung	blue wins

D

datchimsae	closed stance
dobok	uniform
dollyu chagi	roundhouse kick

doobal dangsung   double kick
dui chagi   back kick
duihooryu chagi   spin whip kick
duikoomchi   heel
dukjum   point

H

hoejun   round
  - il hoejun   first round
  - ee hoejun   second round
  - sam hoejun   third round
hogoo   chest protector
hong   red
hong sung   red wins
hooryu chagi   whip kick

J

jayoo kyorugi   free sparring
jirugi   punch
joonbee   ready
jooshim   referee

K

kalyeo   break
kamdokkwan   head of court
kamjum   deduction point
keoman   end
kibon   basic
kihap   yelling
kikwon   withdrawal
kisool   technique
  - kibon kisool   basic technique
  - junmoon kisool   professional technique

kongkyuk   attack
  - kanjup kongkyuk   indirect attack

- jikjup kongkyuk	direct attack
- kiooru kongkyuk	incline attack
- danil kongkyuk	single attack
- mikurro kongkyuk	sliding attack
- jejari kongkyuk	in-place attack
kudup chagi	continous kicking
kulro jitgi	sliding step
kyesok	continue
kyorugi	sparring
kyorumsae	fighting stance
- ap kyorumsae	front fighting stance
- yup kyorumsae	side fighting stance
- ohrun kyorumsae	right handed stance
- woen kyorumsae	left handed stance
kyunggi	competition
kyunggijang	competition site
kyunggi kyuchick	competition rules
kyunggo	warning
kyungrye	bow
kyunggye seon	boundary line

M

machuo kyorugi	arranged sparring
makki	block
- momtong makki	middle section block
- arae makki	low section block
- ulgool makki	high section block
moollu jitgi	back step

N

naeryu chagi	axe kick
naga jitgi	forward step
natchoomsae	low stance

P

panjung	decision
pihagi	avoiding

S

satbodae	protection cup
shigan	time
shihap	competition
shijak	begin
shilkyuk	disqualification
shimpan	judge

W

woosae	superiority

Y

yullimsae	open stance

Appendix B: References

Kukki Taekwondo Kyobon	Kukkiwon	Kukkiwon	1989
International Referee text	WTF	WTF	1992
Sport Theory & Application	Daegun Kim	Sunil Pub.	1988
Elite Sports Training	Hongwon Chae	Bokyng Pub.	1992
Coaching Theory	Jeyun Ku	Hyungsul Pub.	1991
Taekwondo Kyorugi	Yungryul Choi	Samhak Pub.	1989
Taekwondo Quarterly	KTA	KTA	1993
Training Methodology	Jonghoon Kim	Kyohak Pub.	1990
Training Theory	Jimwon Kim	Donghwa Pub.	1988
Living Meditation	Heesun Park	Jungshin Pub.	1992
Sportmassage	BfLW	Wien	1986
For MVP	Mansoo Kang	B & R	1992
Teaching: Way of the Master	Sang H. Kim	Turtle Press	1991
Ultimate Fitness	Sang H. Kim	Turtle Press	1993
Trainingslehre	Harre		1986
Grundlagen des Sportlichen Trainings	Matwejew	Sportverlag	1977
Boxsport	Horst Fiedler	Sportverlag	1980
Judo	Gerhard Lehmann	"	1983
Fechten	Berndt Barth	"	1979
Rinjen	Jurgen Hartmann	"	1980
Leistungssteuerung	M. Grosser	Sportwissen	1986
Konditionstraining	M. Grosser	"	1981
Techniktraining	M. Grosser	"	1986
Riktig Taekwondo	Kyong M. Lee	BLM	1987
Taekwondo	Kyong M. Lee	Alma Press	1989
Combat Strategy	Hanho	Turtle Press	1992

About the Authors

Kuk Hyun Chung

Master Kuk Hyun Chung, considered by many to be the greatest taekwondo competitor ever, won the Gold Medal in Taekwondo in the 1988 Summer Olympic Games. He is listed in the *Guiness Book of Sports Records* as winning the most World Championship titles (1987, 1985, 1983, 1982) by a single person and is undefeated in International Competition. He also won the Athlete's Award in 1984 and 1983 for outstanding performance in competition. He is a graduate of the Korean National College of Physical Education. His latest achievement is the leading role in the 1994 action movie "Taekwon Fighter."

Kyung Myung Lee

Grandmaster Kyung Myung Lee is currently the Deputy Secretary General of the World Taekwondo Federation, headquarters of taekwondo in Seoul, South Korea. He is a 9th degree black belt and author of 5 martial arts books in German, Korean, and Polish. He was the 1988 Olympic coach for the Austrian Olympic Taekwondo Team and chairman of the Technical Committee of the European Taekwondo Association. He is a graduate of Yonsei University.

Sang H. Kim

Master Sang H. Kim is an internationally respected author of 8 martial arts books, including the best sellers *Ultimate Fitness through Martial Arts* and *Teaching: the Way of the Master*, and star of over 50 martial arts instructional videos. He won the 1976 Korean National Champion and was named Instructor of the Year in Korea in 1983. He holds an M.S. degree in physical education and Ph.D. in media studies. He currently devotes his time to teaching and presenting martial arts seminars for students and instructors.

Index

NOTES

Also Available from Turtle Press:

The Martial Arts Training Diary
The Martial Arts Training Diary for Kids
Teaching: The Way of the Master
Combat Strategy
The Art of Harmony
A Guide to Rape Awareness and Prevention
Total MindBody Training
1,001 Ways to Motivate Yourself and Others
Ultimate Fitness through Martial Arts
Weight Training for Martial Artists
Launching a Martial Arts School
Advanced Teaching Report
Hosting a Martial Art Tournament
100 Low Cost Marketing Ideas for the Martial Arts School
A Part of the Ribbon: A Time Travel Adventure
Herding the Ox
Neng Da: Super Punches
250 Ways to Make Classes Fun & Exciting
Martial Arts and the Law
Martial Arts for Women
Parents' Guide to Martial Arts

For more information:
Turtle Press
PO Box 290206
Wethersfield CT 06129-206
1-800-77-TURTL
e-mail: sales@turtlepress.com

http://www.turtlepress.com